CHASING
RABBITS

CHASING RABBITS

Reclaiming God's Plan
For Rest

TIM TWIGG

▶▶▶| ARROW |▶
     P R E S S

Copyright © 2023 Tim Twigg

Any internet addresses (websites, blogs, etc.) in this book are offered as a resource. They are not intended in any way to be or imply an endorsement by Arrow Press Publishing, nor does Arrow Press Publishing vouch for the content of these sites and numbers for the life of this book.

All rights reserved. No part of this publication may be reproduced, distributed, or transmitted in any form or by any means, including photocopying, recording, or other electronic or mechanical methods, without the prior written permission of the publisher, except in the case of brief quotations embodied in critical reviews and certain other noncommercial uses permitted by copyright law. For permission requests, write to the publisher, addressed "Attention: Permissions Coordinator," at the email address: info@arrowpresspublishing.com

Hardcover: 978-1-951475-24-6
Ebook: 978-1-951475-25-3

Library of Congress Control Number:

All Scripture quotations, unless otherwise indicated, are taken from the Holy Bible, New International Version®, NIV®. Copyright ©1973, 1978, 1984, 2011 by Biblica, Inc.™ Used by permission of Zondervan. All rights reserved worldwide. www.zondervan.com. The "NIV" and "New International Version" are trademarks registered in the United States Patent and Trademark Office by Biblica, Inc.™

All Scripture quotations, unless otherwise indicated, are taken from the ESV® Bible (The Holy Bible, English Standard Version®), copyright © 2001 by Crossway, a publishing ministry of Good News Publishers. Used by permission. All rights reserved.

Scripture quotations marked NKJV are taken from the New King James Version®. Copyright © 1982 by Thomas Nelson. Used by permission. All rights reserved.

Scripture quotations marked NLT are taken from the Holy Bible, New Living Translation, copyright ©1996, 2004, 2015 by Tyndale House Foundation. Used by permission of Tyndale House Publishers, a Division of Tyndale House Ministries, Carol Stream, Illinois 60188. All rights reserved.

Scripture quotations marked NIV are taken from the Holy Bible, New International Version®, NIV®. Copyright ©1973, 1978, 1984, 2011 by Biblica, Inc.™ Used by permission of Zondervan. All rights reserved worldwide. www.zondervan.com. The "NIV" and "New International Version" are trademarks registered in the United States Patent and Trademark Office by Biblica, Inc.™

Scripture quotations marked NASB 1995 are from the (NASB®) New American Standard Bible®, Copyright © 1960, 1971, 1977, 1995 by The Lockman Foundation. Used by permission. All rights reserved.

Arrow Press Publishing
Summerville, SC

Dedication

To my amazing wife, thank you for pushing me to rest and find value in the things that really matter.

To every pastor, ministry leader, and volunteer who has put their hand to the plow and not turned back, thank you. The world needs you. Don't burnout. It's time for you to reclaim rest.

CHASING CONTENTS

Shepparton 1

Chaos Addiction 12

Sabbath Silence 32

The Problem of Pride 51

Wait 66

Malnourished 81

Shabbat Shalom 95

It's About Time 106

Shepparton Revisited 116

Endnotes 119

SHEPPARTON

CHAPTER ONE

"A person who chases two rabbits, catches neither."
– Confucius

The race began like every other race at the Shepparton Greyhound Racing Club in Kialla, Victoria, Australia. Ginny Lou, a lean, sleek, muscular greyhound, shot out of the gate, eager to catch that rascally rabbit who always sped just beyond her reach.

Modern greyhound racing is said to have been formed in 1919, with the invention of the mechanical lure. Today, this mechanical lure can be as simple as a bone or as complex as a rabbit-shaped form covered with fake fur. The racing dogs never know the difference between a real rabbit and the fake one because it is there to chase, not catch. The mechanical hare is electronically controlled and propelled around the track, close enough to catch but always out of reach.

But this particular race was not like every other race. The unexpected happened. As the dogs ran, a real rabbit unexpectedly darted onto the track. Most of the them continued chasing the mechanical rabbit as usual, but one dog, Ginny Lou, diverted from the course to pursue the real thing.[1]

I have to wonder if the other dogs looked judgmentally at Ginny Lou as she ran wildly after the real bunny and thought, *Doesn't she realize it's now impossible for her to win this race?*

Meanwhile, I imagine Ginny Lou looked bewildered at the other dogs chasing the mechanical rabbit and thought, *Don't they realize they're chasing after something that's not real?*

Every day, millions of people chase after things that don't matter. They run after fabricated success, advancement, and financial gain like greyhounds after a mechanical lure. It's not that those things aren't important. It's not that they lack value. The problem is they hold no value in light of eternity. In fact, they

Chasing Rabbits

may not even hold value a decade later. Or even next year. Yet we chase after them, and we do so with militant zeal.

Much like the greyhounds at Shepparton, we also chase after rabbits. Chances are, it's not an actual rabbit, although that no doubt happens. I'm referring to the metaphorical rabbit, the "thing" we believe will make our life better. The "thing" for which we're willing to sacrifice our health, our family, and our destiny. The "thing," that, when caught, will leave us surprisingly unfulfilled.

Yet, there is good news. God has given us a remedy for all of the rabbit chasing. He gave us a directive and a promise. He gave us the hope of rest. He gave us the Sabbath.

What Is the Sabbath?

In his book *The Sabbath*, Jewish theologian Abraham Joshua Heschel expands on this concept, likening it to a conflict between space and time. Space being the physical trappings of life —the mountains of stuff we acquire year after year—and time being the commodity we spend to acquire space.[2] God, in His infinite wisdom, understood we are not capable of working without end, so He instituted the law, the command, the kindness of the Sabbath.

God has asked us to take time, one day every week, and devote it to Him, with the desire that we emphasize time, not space. Intimacy, not accumulation. Yet we don't. We choose to work every day, giving little yield to the first thing He called holy, the Sabbath, and instead sacrifice the resplendent moments of intermission that unite us deeply with the Holy Spirit. Heschel comments:

He who wants to enter the holiness of the day must first lay down the profanity of clattering commerce, of being yoked to toil. He must go away from the screech of dissonant days, from the nervousness and fury of acquisitiveness and the betrayal in embezzling his own life. He must say farewell to manual work and learn to understand that the world has already been created and will survive without the help of man. Six days a week we wrestle with the world, wringing profit from the earth; on the Sabbath we especially care for the seed of eternity planted in the soul. The world has our hands, but our soul belongs to Someone Else. Six days a week we seek to dominate the world, on the seventh day we try to dominate the self.[3]

God asks us to take 14.29 percent of our week and do . . . not . . . work. He requests that we commune with Him in prayer, worship, and presence instead. He asks us to commit our hearts to think on Him, meditate on His Word, and, more importantly, experience supernatural rest. He asks us to stop chasing the mechanical rabbit for one day and allow ourselves to be refreshed by the real thing.

The Need for a Sabbath

Honoring the Sabbath is a simple yet difficult-to-follow request. Many people believe rest to be a waste of time—hours upon hours of doing nothing, accomplishing nothing, and experiencing nothing, frittered away, when they could achieve so much more.

But time, wisdom, and suffering force us to modulate our perspective on the matter of rest. Older age also has a way of magnifying rest in a way a young person seldom tolerates. In our youth we maximize the energy of our budding minds and minimize the efficiency of patient observances. "I'll rest when I'm dead," we boldly proclaim, not realizing the expediency of such an unfortunate outcome. Few want this permanent rest, and even fewer are eternally prepared for it.

To rest is admittedly counterintuitive, not to the body but to ambition. Ambition willingly sacrifices the vessel of productivity for accolades and applause. Ambition howls, "Carpe diem!" as it carelessly trots toward burnout, declining health, and irreparable relational deterioration.

Accomplishment and ambition are not teammates. Despite what we may believe, they do not benefit each other. Accomplishment is never permanent, and ambition is never satisfied. Neither can be enjoyed in the present, and both lose purpose if they remain unshared. Ambition may create temporary feelings of accomplishment, but if we relish in accomplishment too long, life leaves us behind. If we settle into a static state of ambition, what accomplishments we do achieve shrivel away when measured against what we gave away to achieve them. The losses always weigh heavier later in life.

For most of my working life, I paid no regard to the holiness of the Sabbath. Since graduating from college, I've always had two jobs. I even worked seventy to eighty hours a week for over four years. Now, I look back on my naiveté and shake my head in disapproval. I remember the stress. I remember the imbalance. I remember how it caused me to falter mentally, spiritually, and relationally. Everything revolved around work. For several years I worked two jobs while also completing multiple

Chasing Rabbits

graduate degrees. I never took a day off. And in doing so, I learned a very painful truth.

Sin feasts on exhaustion.

Our guard drops and we make poor decisions. When we refuse to be refreshed in God's presence, seasons lose their meaning. There is no pause. There is no respite. There is only "go," and the faulty proposition of a never-ending string of days that will rob the worth from every bit of toil we can muster.

Rest may be counterintuitive to our flesh, but it is perfectly harmonious with our spirit. Rest hydrates the soul with dreams, creativity, health, and spiritual vitality. It is unparalleled in its rejuvenation of our physical bodies, and, more importantly, through our observance of rest as a spiritual discipline, we find a greater, mystical experience. God seeks to interact with the highest-functioning version of us. Our bodies, while sin riddled and unredeemable apart from Jesus's sacrifice, have an optimal operational setting that is driven by time, not ambition. Rest is not suggested but required. Lack of rest causes irritability, confusion, and even hallucinations and irrational actions. The optimal setting mandates daily observances in the form of naps and sleep, as well as weekly observances in the form of a Sabbath.

Yet, time carries within its structure a certain level of temptation. The enemy persistently seeks to rob us of our time or distract us into wasting it on frivolous activity. This or that, we must choose, and every choice carries with it a chronological cost, the price of which we are seldom able to pay.

Our mortality demands rest, yet soul rest will not happen without intention. The power of rest should be maximized, should be purposeful, and should hold great spiritual value. Rest will also position us to hear Holy Spirit clearer, empower us to exploit our strength deposits to follow His promptings, and allow us to discover a world where ambition is less profitable than accomplishment born from His presence.

My prayer is that our commitment to rest is not found in the form of a temporary respite, but a deep-seated celebration of tranquility. The Sabbath is not idealistic. It is our inheritance. It is a gift. It is an endowment of honor and holiness through which we can start anew.

Chasing What Matters

What we chase matters. So does how we chase it. It's not about movement, it's about moments. It's about surrendering pride, redirecting passion, and repurposing space and time to encounter the Eternal One.

When we chase after what matters, we apply boundaries to assist us in reaching the goal. Furthermore, we lean into those who would help us accomplish our objective. Why the Sabbath? Because the Lord knew what we'd need to succeed, and work without end means falling short of the goal.

In Exodus 20, sandwiched between the first three commandments, which instruct us how we are to relate to God, and the final six commandments, which guide us in how we relate to each other, is the fourth commandment:

> Six days you shall labor and do all your work, but the seventh day is the Sabbath of the Lord your God. In it you shall do no work: you, nor your son, nor your daughter, nor your male servant, nor your female servant, nor your cattle, nor your stranger who is within your gates. For in six days the Lord

made the heavens and the earth, the sea, and all that is in them, and rested the seventh day. Therefore the Lord blessed the Sabbath day and hallowed it. (vv. 9–11 NKJV)

Here, God tells the Israelites, His people newly liberated from slavery in Egypt, to remember and keep the Sabbath. Some theologians insist that the terminology here, to keep the Sabbath holy, indicates it was holy long before this sacred moment when the first download was made onto a tablet.

The first mention of a Sabbath day is found in Exodus 16. It was a novel concept, and one that God's people initially had trouble grasping. Yet, the Sabbath was not intended to limit their success, but exactly the opposite. God provided His people bread from heaven in the form of manna and then told them to rest.

We really need to grasp this concept. His people were grumbling and complaining, and God's answer was not to put them to work, but to provide for them and encourage them to rest. What God had created was good. It was a place for humankind to work and also to rest in Him. When Adam and Eve disobeyed in the garden of Eden, they surrendered everything they had come to take for granted. From that moment until Exodus 16, humankind operated in survival mode. Now God was raining down manna to meet their needs, giving them a glimpse of His glorious covenant, an invitation to return to the garden for one day a week and find their rest in Him.

Pursuing Divine Rest

This book your holding is about the Sabbath. It's about the beauty of kingdom accomplishment by doing less. It's about honoring time with God over unnecessary accumulation. It's a treasure chest filled not with gold, but broken clocks, showing us that we no longer have to yield to the demands of the world, even if for one day a week. As it turns out, one day has always been enough to prepare our hearts for what lies ahead.

That said, the Sabbath is not a magical elixir. If we choose to pursue divine rest, we will find ourselves facing excessive temptation beckoning us to a life fraught with insatiable ambition. No, the Sabbath is not easy, but it is unavoidably necessary. It is not the reward at the end of the journey, but the banquet before the journey begins. It is the nourishment before the expenditure of energy. God created the universe and then demonstrated shabbat; He ceased to create. In this moment, born from His Sabbath, came our mandate to continue the cause of creation—not physical worlds or alternate universes, but worlds within worlds and universes within universes. We create tables from trees and batteries from lithium.

There are no limits to our creativity, but there are limits to our productivity. No matter how brilliant, how driven, or how passionate we are about what we are creating, we must succumb to the siren song called rest or our creative acts will come to a violent halt.

We may clumsily claim that the antidote to being without is to acquire more, not to evaluate our work but to consume more of it. Yet, spiritual lack has never been satisfied by carnal abundance. The gravity of more leads us to irreverent action.

Chasing Rabbits

On the seventh day, God rested. He ceased work, and in so doing He modeled the path of bringing toil to completion. Work is not a substitute for His presence, and if toil has distracted us from intimacy, it's time to re-evaluate what we are chasing. Ginny Lou the greyhound was able to spot the real from the fake. She was able to determine the futile pursuit from a chase that mattered, and she was a dog.

If she can do it, so can we.

There remains, then, a Sabbath-rest for the people of God; for anyone who enters God's rest also rests from their works, just as God did from his.

Hebrews 4:9–10 NIV

CHAOS ADDICTION

CHAPTER TWO

"I accept chaos. I'm not sure whether or not it accepts me."
– Bob Dylan

"I'll bet you can't put salt on the rabbit's tail!" John shouted.

John was responsible for groundskeeping at our small church in New Jersey. A rabbit would occasionally scurry across his path and in this instance, he took the opportunity to incite Tommy, my older brother. Accepting the provocation, Tommy ran into the house, grabbed the salt shaker, and bolted out the door. He ran as fast as his four-year-old legs would take him, desperately trying to catch the evasive brown-and-white bunny. I was only two years old at the time, so I don't remember the ordeal, but my mother and father fondly tell the story often. It must have been cutely chaotic to watch him chase a rabbit.

The four-year-old version of my brother had no limits. There were seemingly no tasks he couldn't accomplish and no challenges he couldn't overcome, so chasing after a rabbit to put salt on its tail seemed like a perfectly reasonable idea. After running until exhausted, he eventually gave up. He embraced the harsh reality that no matter how hard he tried, much like the mechanical lure to a greyhound, he wouldn't be able to put salt on the rabbit's tail.

The wild rabbit always runs away from a potential threat, never toward it. You'll never stroll through the woods and have a bunny jump into your arms to snuggle. It's not natural. Chaos can be fascinating to observe but exhausting to experience. Chaos is oddly enticing this way. Sabbath is our solution to soul sucking chaos.

Chaos and the Sabbath

A great many things naturally go together. Macaroni and cheese. Bacon and eggs. Milk and cookies. Fish and chips. The

Cleveland Browns and losing seasons.

"Chaos and the Sabbath" would not make this list. To accept one is to eradicate the other. They don't blend well, play well, or produce positive results. One must dominate; there are no half-measures. A little chaos never remains a little chaos. Just as peace prevails in the presence of God, unrest triumphs in times of chaos.

Peace and unrest are also options in moments of failure. My brother never put salt on the rabbit's tail, but he didn't dwell on that failure. He quickly moved on and played with his toys. You may say, "Well, that's easy for a child. It's what they're supposed to do," but I think it's what we should do too. Choosing peace amid failure-bred chaos is a healthy choice, but we are chronically unhealthy. We throw more chaos into the fray and hope two negatives produce a positive.

Observing the Sabbath shrinks the tumor called chaos and surgically removes its effect on our conscience.

Memories of failure can sear into our psyche. When this happens, we form two responses to future challenges. Either we'll try harder, innovate more, and work later into the night, or we'll give up, conceding to the lamentable reality that the goal is unattainable.

Those who try harder and strive for greater productivity may convince themselves that they'll finally achieve what was previously thought to be unachievable. Productive people often exist in this prolonged state of intensity, so much so that when the intensity wanes, so does their self-worth. Everything is tightly tied to the excessive collision of purpose and chaos. Chaos is no longer looked upon as a negative development that threatens harmony; it becomes the goal.

Chasing Rabbits

Chaos, left unchecked and unobstructed, does not emerge from its chrysalis in the form of a majestic butterfly. Neglected chaos will never breed anything beautiful, at least not without an outside influence to shape its uncertainty into order. Only an infinite God can form creation from chaos, order from entropy. We try to assume a divine role in settling chaos. but our emotional, relational, and carnal imperfections never allow permanent stability.

When chaos leads us, restlessness, excitement, and drama adhere to our personality and purpose. We find reasons to avoid rest, spend exorbitant amounts of money on thrill-seeking adventures, and foster relational tensions under the guise of advancement. We force positive views of chaos through unhealthy lenses.

Now, I'm not referring to elements of chaos, but a lifestyle of chaos. Momentary chaos can bring about unity in the workforce, strengthen character, spark creativity, and solidify vision. According to Ashli Akins in her TEDx talk, *The Creativity of Chaos*, "Without chaos we are too stable to reorganize. We are too inflexible to adapt and change."[1] It seems chaos is necessary for spiritual, relational, and professional metamorphosis. But then there are disturbances.

Disturbances in Life

Disturbances can often be mistaken for chaos because they look the same in their provenance. Both chaos and disturbances unsettle order and deface any semblance of peace. Chaos, however, is unpredictable and cannot produce a calculable outcome. It is anarchic in nature. Anarchic, but not necessarily evil.

Chasing Rabbits

God existed before any created thing, and that means He allowed formlessness before creation. He allowed chaos to exist and then transformed it into something resplendent—something beautiful that reflected His character. Chaos is ground zero for the creative explosion. Its aftermath, when formed by the Creator, is not destruction but an established order that points to His goodness. Every created thing is a reflection of Him.

When we're confronted with a fickle force such as chaos, our insecurities surface and we fight two battles simultaneously. We are besieged with doubt and assailed with the weight of the creative act. Chaos can latch onto our souls and drive us mad with misguided pretension. The Creator wrangled chaos in six days, completed His creation, and rested on the seventh day. We are not God, but we are called to follow His lead. We must attack chaos with extreme barbarity for six days, then turn our back and cast our gaze on the Creator on the seventh. By doing this, we find not only rest but also a spiritually restored mind, brimming with neoteric ideas fresh from God's assembly line.

In contrast, disturbances can be intentional. They can be methodical. Disturbances can fashion a positive outcome from a negative occasion. A disturbance is a detour. Yet, when expediency is the priority, detours are seen as an inconvenience.

The truth is, nobody likes a road detour, even if it is for our benefit. It lengthens the time needed to get to our destination. A detour often means there is work ahead or danger ahead. Either way, proceeding down the path will result in harm to your car, your person, or to someone else. A detour is an intentional disturbance for the protection of the driver. This type of disturbance is a great benefit to us.

Chasing Rabbits

God creates disturbances in our lives all the time. Whenever we invite Holy Spirit to guide and direct us, we declare our willingness to embrace disturbances as necessary by an infinitely kind, loving, and protective Father. Disturbances cause us to refocus, lean in, and embrace our insufficiency. They also stir our faith, as we never know how long the detour will take, what we'll encounter along the way, or whether we'll have enough strength to survive the trek. Yet, we need not fear disturbances, nor do we need to create them. Disturbances will come and go as life allots them, but for the person who is in Christ, disturbances carry with them a future glory.

Paul spoke of this future glory in Romans 8:18–30. *All* of creation groans under the weight of disorder (v. 22). Just as the Spirit of God hovered over the unformed earth, so He hovers over our unformed lives, shaping order from chaos, holiness from depravity, and righteousness from degenerate thoughts and deeds. He intercedes for us (v. 27), brings good from tragedy (v. 28), and gives hope through faith (v. 24).

The Disturbance of the Sabbath

The Sabbath is also a disturbance. For six days we create. We take the flawed, exhausted, fragile world around us and attempt to produce something beautiful. Six days a week we toil, scrape, and claw our way through immense amounts of uncertainty, fear, and spiritual warfare, with the hope that our labor will make sense of our existence. We struggle to create order from chaos, using every tool within our reach.

Some days we succeed. When we lie down at night, we feel accomplished. Purposeful. Fulfilled. Satisfied. Those are the days when order wins over chaos. Then there are the days when we succumb to the rat race. We interweave pride and selfish ambition with eternal squabbles over progress and promotion. Nothing is ever good enough on those days, and those days lead to those nights. Sleeplessness, confusion, and hopelessness. We don't like those days, and we like those nights even less. To avoid them, we pledge our allegiance to more work, not less. We don't regroup, we reload. We multiply dysfunction, obtain the same results, and do it again. And again. And again. And again.

We struggle with God's grace and mercy in a similar way. We feel we must toil for forgiveness. Surely, receiving such an incomparable gift such as salvation mandates an industrial barter. We think we must work to repay what we did not earn, could not earn, and never deserved to begin with. But how silly of us to think of God in terms of repayment. How can we repay someone who will never be without? How can we give back to someone who has never lacked? How can we insist on providing for someone who has never known need?

Our earthly achievements mean nothing to God. Our houses, cars, and bank accounts are temporal, sublunary efforts to assign value to our existence. All the while, God simply desires us. Our engagement. Intimacy. Love. Not that any of these things would bring completeness to Him; He is complete unto Himself. The disturbance of the Sabbath adds value to us, not to Him. In the moments of cessation, He removes the scales of achievement and whispers, "I am enough."

The Sabbath confronts our chaos addiction with abundant grace and barbarous honesty. Repeatedly practicing the Sabbath resets our ambitions. The disturbance of the Sabbath brings clarity. Peace. Honesty. The Sabbath is more than a rote submission to laziness; it is casting our intentional gaze on the Sufficient One, finding ourselves sufficient in Him, and resting by still waters so that our souls would be restored (Psalm 23).

Solemn Rest

Leviticus 23:3 exhorts us, "Six days shall work be done, but on the seventh day is a Sabbath of solemn rest, a holy convocation. You shall do no work. It is a Sabbath to the Lord in all your dwelling places."

Solemn, serious rest. A holy meeting with the Lord. This is our reward, not our punishment. Is not rest the goal of work? Do we not work to earn enough money to take a vacation? To take days off? To retire? Work brings purpose, but it also brings stress to achieve an ideal end to our lives. We work to gain options, but we rest to gain perspective.

You may experience guilt and anxiety as you detox from chaos. At first, fulfilling the Sabbath may feel more irksome than serene. It may feel like the detour, the disturbance, keeping you from accomplishing your goals. In reality, it is God re-introducing you to His goals, His ambitions, and His purpose. Honoring the Sabbath gives you proper perspective for the other six days, allowing you to toil with persistence but not permanence.

As God spoke to me about the grace given through the Sabbath, a new set of tensions arose within me. My family had been used to living a certain way for quite some time, so my personal commitment to honoring the Sabbath caused an unexpected disruption in my home. Schedules had to be rearranged, lines had to be drawn, and challenging conversations had to occur so that we kept our pursuit of Yahweh the priority. It was a clumsy start, and it still has its tense moments. A settling had to occur, much like the foundation of a new home. At first, it felt unreasonable. Chaos seemed to increase, not decrease, but that should come as no surprise. This is what happens when you endeavor to forcibly magnify your spirit and crucify your flesh. As I said, chaos is anarchic.

The conflict of flesh and spirit is a conflict of power and authority. Power is the ability to do. Authority is the ability to determine. You may have the power to perform an action, but not the authority to do so. In Christ we have been given authority, but only as we submit to His authority (James 4:7). The transfer of authority is not rooted in meritocracy. The authority given to us is not based on our abilities apart from the Holy Spirit. It comes only after the repentant heart responds to conviction and reunites us with God through the sacrifice of Jesus Christ. In that moment, God does not just grant us power (Acts 1:8); He also endues us with authority (Luke 10:19; 9:1; Matthew 28:18–20;18:18–20; 2 Corinthians 10:3–5) to appropriately use the power in hand, as well as the wisdom to understand the timing of our determinations.

As a follower of Jesus, we have both the power and authority to command our flesh to follow Holy Spirit. It must come into alignment with the Creator. It has no choice. When the Sabbath comes, our flesh will war. There is so much to be done, so many unchecked boxes on the to-do list, so many needs that have nothing to do with rest, and, in fact, are impeded by such a day.

If we could only grasp the paradoxical duality of the Sabbath. It both regenerates and slays. It regards and revolts. While honoring the Sabbath brings spiritual health and vitality, it also destroys the carnality within, but we need not worry about the fallout because we experience restoration within the obedient act.

Hidden Implications of Chaos

Chaos has communal implications. It refuses to live in isolation. By nature, chaos is a gatherer, inviting all to join in its destructive ambitions. Ironically, we are more deliberate with eradicating chaos found in others than we are in ourselves. We look at the chaos in our schools, state, and country, but seldom take time to address the chaos within.

Professor Jordan Peterson took note of this in his book *12 Rules for Life: An Antidote to Chaos*. He says, "Don't reorganize the state until you have ordered your own experience. Have some humility. If you cannot bring peace to your household, how dare you try to rule a city?"[2]

Paul said it this way: "For if someone does not know how to manage his own household, how will he care for God's church?" (1 Timothy 3:5). This was a qualification for leading God's Bride. Order, not chaos. Individual order invites communal order, which leads to national order. We mistakenly think macro before micro. We want to apply large-scale philosophies of global order before we have worked them out in our own homes. Yet order must be established, and it must be done by invoking He who has never been out of order.

God is not a God of confusion, but of peace (1 Corinthians 14:33). His plans are right and His purposes pure. God is patient with us because He is never surprised by us. He is never scared. He is never frantic. On the contrary, He tells us to be anxious about nothing (Philippians 4:6), fear not (Isaiah 41:10), and have

Chasing Rabbits

faith, without which it would be impossible to please Him (Hebrews 11:16). Any good child wants to please their parents, yet deliberate disobedience is not pleasing. Deliberate disobedience that leads to suffering is even less pleasing. It's frustrating when a child suffers because they didn't listen to instruction.

Rebellion, though, is an unfortunate theme for humanity. It is the birthplace of chaos, as chaos cannot breathe in an atmosphere of obedience. Rebellion welcomes destruction, and an evil person seeks after it (Proverbs 17:11). When the Holy Spirit is present, order follows. It may be worth mentioning that order does not always mean comfort, nor does it mean a life free from disturbance. Order means things are as they should be in a perfected sense; they cannot be any other way.

The Need for Order and Obedience

Order can feel like chaos if we allow our flesh to hold center stage. Far too many allow disorder to be their established norm, even drawing their identity from their rebellious acts. Proud of what they have become, they let chaos gradually dismantle every relationship until only a pile of nuts and bolts remain, the evidence of the once-upon-a-time construction of achievement.

Order must be attained, chaos must be limited, and obedience must prevail if we ever hope to experience the rest God promises, both temporally and eternally.

Maintaining internal order amid external chaos is quite hard. Obeying the voice of the Father when we're bombarded with the chaotic is seldom easy, yet obedience is exactly what God requires, not for His benefit but for ours.

One of the most heartbreaking stories in the Bible is when King Saul was confronted with the result of his disobedience. The prophet Samuel informed King Saul, "For rebellion is as the sin of divination, and presumption is as iniquity and idolatry. Because you have rejected the word of the Lord, He has rejected you from being king" (1 Samuel 15:23).

Without knowing the context, it appears Saul was simply being a good steward. He was instructed to destroy Amalek and everything he owned, including the livestock. Saul, however, chose chaos. The command was clear, God's directives decipherable, and His purpose plain, yet Saul chose chaos. All reasons are irrational in light of the Lord's commands. "He has turned back from following me and has not performed my commandments," lamented the Lord (v. 11). But

Saul believed he'd nailed it. "I have performed the commandment of the Lord," he proudly exclaimed to the prophet Samuel the following day (v. 13).

Samuel asked, "What then is this bleating of the sheep in my ears and the lowing of the oxen that I hear?" (v. 14), to which Saul answered, "They have brought them from the Amalekites for the people spared the best of the sheep and of the oxen to sacrifice to the Lord your God, and the rest we have devoted to destruction" (v. 15).

I wonder if Saul's verbiage —"the Lord your God"—had anything to do with his disobedience. Perhaps if it had been "the Lord my God," he would not have been in this predicament. Perhaps if he had submitted himself to the authority of the Lord, he would have not felt the need to assert his own power.

Half-obedience is complete rebellion. Rebellion produces chaos, which results in rejection and then ends in hopeless isola-

Chasing Rabbits

tion. It's an impeccable recipe for a crushed spirit. The enemy thrives in chaos and multiplies its offspring. Saul not only invited others into the chaos; he also blamed them for the defiance. "They did it," he excused the behavior. "And they did it for God." I imagine Samuel saying, "Are you telling me that you disobeyed God, you are blaming the people you lead, and this disregard of His command was for His benefit?"

Saul was quite deceived as he chased his rabbits. Rebellion cloaked in honor and stewardship may work with imperfect people, but it will never prevail before a perfect, holy God. Samuel's response has been echoed across so many situations: "Has the Lord as great delight in burnt offerings and sacrifices, as in obeying the voice of the Lord? Behold, to obey is better than sacrifice, and to listen than the fat of rams" (v. 22).

We embrace chaos by ignoring the commands of the Lord, and there is no acceptable excuse to do otherwise. His command for a Sabbath is no different. Let's look at a few excuses, some of which you may have used.

- I have to work on my Sabbath or I'll lose my job.
- I need the overtime to help me get out of debt so I can give more to God.
- I'll only work a little bit. I'm not going to work a full day.
- I use my Sabbath to work for the Lord.
- I'm so busy, I need to work on my day off just to catch up.
- I can't sit still; I'm not wired that way (one of my personal greatest hits).
- I'll rest when I'm dead.
- Rise and grind! God honors those who do for themselves.

- If you don't work, you don't eat! That's what the Bible says!

By embracing these excuses, we rebel against the One we're claiming to please. Let's pull back the veil of deception, as Samuel did, and bring truth to those arguments.

- Deep down, we don't believe He is our provider.
- We're using the command to give as an excuse to break the law.
- A little disobedience is still disobedience and carries with it the same penalty.
- We're too busy to be spiritually healthy.
- We'll never catch up when our priorities are imbalanced.
- God's commands have nothing to do with our personality or physical "wiring."
- Without rest, we'll be dead sooner than we think.
- God honors those who obey Him. Period.
- If we try to manipulate His Word for our benefit, we'll receive King Saul's reward.

God's commands are not subject to debate. His commands offer no room for our interpretation of fairness. When confronted with his sin, Saul begged for redirection. He invited chaos, God's rejection, and his impending removal as king of Israel, and it was more than he could handle. He was broken, but as is the result of chaos, the brokenness did not fall on him alone. Samuel grieved over Saul; he wept for him.

I imagine Samuel back at his home, pacing back and forth, shouting in frustration, "Why couldn't he just listen? This could

Chasing Rabbits

have all been avoided if he had just done what God had said!" Saul's rebellion led to chaos in the kingdom, and chaos for his successor, David.

I ask these same questions when I see the exhausted, burned out, and weary. Why is it they don't listen to God's commandment to rest? Don't they realize they can accomplish more in six days with rest than seven days without? Don't they realize this could all be avoided?

It is in the tranquility of the Sabbath we discover that this disruptive day is a gift for our development. For Saul, it should have been better to have no sheep but to obey the Lord. It's better to have nothing and live in obedience than to have abundance without favor.

We inevitably invite chaos when we rebel against the Sabbath. We may even glorify our rebellion. As a pastor, I could certainly give way to the busyness of the calling, pretending the Father approves because we are, after all, doing His work. How preposterous. Would I approve of my daughter working without rest on my behalf? Of course not. I would implore her to refrain. As a dad, I would insist on it, and settle for no excuse in contrast. Busyness has never been an acceptable excuse for disobedience.

The Problem with Busyness

One could mistakenly think spiritual leaders have a better handle on observing the Sabbath, as if work was solely a secular concept. Pastor and author Eugene Peterson spoke of the busy pastor this way: "The one piece of mail certain to go unread into my wastebasket is the one addressed to the busy pastor. Not that the phrase doesn't describe me at times, but I refuse to give my attention to someone who encourages what is worst in me."[3]

I'm not arguing the accuracy of *busy*; I am, though, contesting the way it is used to flatter and express sympathy. "The poor pastor," we say. "So devoted to his flock; the work is endless and he sacrifices himself so unstintingly." But *busy* is the symptom not of commitment but of betrayal, not devotion but defection. The word, set as a modifier to *pastor*, should sound to our ears like *adulterous* to characterize a wife, or *embezzling* to describe a banker. It is an outrageous scandal, a blasphemous affront.

Eugene Peterson provided two reasons for a busy pastor: either vanity or laziness. They are vain in that their significance makes them feel important, or lazy in that they allow others to determine their activity for them.[4]

I believe these descriptors apply to everyone, not just pastors, and they certainly apply to those who refuse the Sabbath. One must be insistent to their family, friends, and coworkers that the Sabbath is not to be ignored. They must not be lazy. They must set their schedule, their precious meeting time with the Lord, and position themselves to hear from Him. To be forthright in obedience is not rude, but it will be offensive to some. It will disturb their sensibilities and their conscience. They may feel conviction for not setting aside this holy time themselves, but do not waver. Chaos has an antidote. It is, and has always been, creation and toil followed by rest.

In joyful times, we seldom wonder whether God is with us. I believe we think little about His presence in the peacetimes because our soul tells us this is exactly how life should be. Peace, joy, prosperity, love. They are our birthright, prior to the Adamic fall. Joy-filled moments are an outpouring of a perfect future into

Chasing Rabbits

our imperfect present. They are the moments when all seems right with the world.

You know those moments—the peace and the miracle. For some it's the soft breeze while sitting on the beach, watching their children laugh and play. For others it is the rhythmic tick of a grandfather clock while they sip on a cup of coffee. No matter what may get you there, your soul longs for those moments, and in times of turmoil, your soul fights, kicks, and claws to get back to them.

Troubled times—those are the times when we doubt His concern, even His existence. Chaos shocks and confuses our souls. We then question our ideologies, in search of a reality that makes sense. But chaos doesn't make sense. Suffering often has no rationale. No dogma brings true peace. Soulful reprieve is only found in Jesus. And if it's only found in Him, then He is truly the best we could hope to have.

But if He is truly the best we could hope to have, why would we not strive to have Him more?

Sabbath's Remedy for Chaos

Can chaos ever be good? Certainly, in that the chaos is directed toward disorder. Ironically, order feels very much like chaos to anarchism. A life of disorder, when presented with structure, planning, and accountability, may feel more like a prison than a spiritual encounter. If disorder is commonplace, consider chaos a necessary disruption and embrace it as a gift for your development.

You may think nobody likes chaos, but I believe nobody likes other people's chaos. We are quite fine with our own disor-

Chasing Rabbits

der, or at least we learn to tolerate our disorders while judgmentally criticizing others. Look at hoarders. According to the International OCD Foundation, compulsive hoarding includes all three of the following:

- A person collects and keeps a lot of items, even things that appear useless or of little value to most people, and
- These items clutter the living spaces and keep the person from using their rooms as they were intended, and
- These items cause distress or problems in day-to-day activities.[5]

The outcome of compulsive hoarding is ongoing stress, yet compulsive hoarders have embraced the disorder and may even insist that hoarding doesn't affect their lives at all. Chaos entered their home and they fixed it a meal and allowed it to stay rent-free.

People may say, "What is wrong with having stuff? Stuff isn't bad." And that's true, but possession is a moving target. One moment we own things, the next moment they own us. One never knows when the threshold has been crossed until it's too late, and everyone's threshold is different. Consistency isn't found in the violation, but in the outcome.

- Severe clutter threatens the health and safety of those living in or near the home, causing health problems, structural damage, fire, and even death.
- Expensive and emotionally devastating evictions or other court actions can lead to hospitalizations or homelessness.

Chasing Rabbits

- Conflict erupts with family members and friends who are frustrated and concerned about the state of the home and the hoarding behaviors.[6]

True rest cannot be found in stuff, and it most certainly cannot be found in sustained chaos. We must get our home in order, and this order must be holistic. Sustained chaos in professional, relational, and spiritual environments cannot be allowed. Chaos will never fully leave us. Like sin, it is always crouching at our door, waiting for the opportune time to wreck our world. This is why a consistent, weekly Sabbath is nonnegotiable. It stays the swarms of uncertainty. It refocuses the erratic soul. It refreshes the spiritually parched.

In observing the Sabbath, we are painting a portrait of spiritual order, of six passably productive days and one that's torrential with meaning. Chaos is not our friend, and neither is the rabbit we're frantically chasing with the salt shaker. It's time to pause, return to the presence of God, and chase after Him instead. Unlike the rabbit, He wants to be caught by us.

SABBATH SILENCE

CHAPTER THREE

"If you don't think, you shouldn't talk!"
– March Hare, Alice in Wonderland

Silence is not lewd or irreverent, but it can be unkind. Many a wide-eyed adolescent has felt the passive-aggressive sting of the "cold shoulder." Sadly, it's a manipulative weapon in the toolbox of adults as well. Silence is amoral but can be yielded to hurt deeply. If you have experienced the rejection of a child, a parent, or another loved one, and they have cut themselves off from any and all communication, you surely understand the disconcerting ache for conversation.

Silence is not the enemy. To eradicate silence would be to force premature healing and humility. Like with a broken leg not properly set, the long-term negative implications are unavoidable. Patience is needed for silence to accomplish its work, and in the hand of a master communicator, silence is a powerful tool indeed.

No one communicates better than the Holy Spirit, but there are moments when silence is the only message to be heard. This can be uncomfortable if your faith has never outgrown the crib. The question then becomes, how can one enjoy silence? Should silence be vital when observing the Sabbath? My question is, why shouldn't it be? Is there something about silence so repulsive that it should be avoided at all costs? Perhaps, but it has little to do with silence. Silence clarifies our thoughts—the thoughts we have attempted to crowd out with incessant work and noise.

Silence and the Sabbath

During the Sabbath, we must slow down to hear the guidance of the Holy Spirit, but such guidance is not simply directional; it is metamorphic. When we sit in silence to hear His voice, when we earnestly pray Psalm 139 and ask Him to bring

Chasing Rabbits

to our consciousness our subliminal depravity, and when we take one step closer to Him—that's when we are overwhelmed with the perilousness of our sin. Many of us go to great lengths to avoid confronting the part of us that displeases the Lord, to find ourselves in silence's shadow unable to evade the reality of imperfection.

Silence's goal is not to humiliate or defeat us. It desires to bring our impurities to the surface for God to masterfully remove, restoring our soul and our connection with Him.

Should silence be vital to Sabbath observance? Yes. It is not a day of silence, but an hour of silence may feel like a day when you exit the world's highway of distraction, fear, unmet expectations, dysfunction, and degradation. As you regularly Sabbath, you'll find yourself yearning for silence's cathartic scalpel.

Silence: Blessing or Curse?

God had a great deal of work to do in the Israelites' lives as they journeyed from Egypt's bondage to the Promised Land. One would think the lure of freedom and the fulfilled promise of liberation would be far greater than the seduction of excess, yet it wasn't long before the groans of lack filled the air and putrefied His blessing: "If only we had died by the Lord's hand in Egypt! There we sat around pots of meat and ate all the food we wanted, but you have brought us out into this desert to starve this entire assembly for death" (Exodus 16:4 NIV).

A bit dramatic, and perhaps a touch manipulative in the delivery, was this emotionally charged statement. The assembly was chasing a promise, and in that moment, the promise felt empty. The all-powerful God who had done the impossible in

Egypt seemed to struggle with feeding the free. To be fair, trust was a new concept for this group of people. Four hundred and thirty years of oppression and forced submission had robbed Israel of their faith. They knew what it meant to be submitted to an earthly master, and while it immense physical and psychological pain, the potted meat and reliability of their cruel oppressors were at least known. God, while good, kind, and benevolent in all His ways, was a stranger.

Today, Israel gets lambasted for their grumbling and complaining in the wilderness by well-meaning, albeit pious, Christians. We flip a few pages and question how they could possibly doubt God after He freed them from Egypt in such a miraculous way.

How could they doubt? Four hundred and thirty years of silence, that's how.

Israel relied on oral tradition to tell them of God's heroics, but they didn't know the Lord. And not much has changed since then. According to recent Barna research, just over one-third of US adults (34 percent) read the Bible once a week or more, while half (50 percent) read the Bible less than twice a year (including never).[1] We hear of God in movies and through stories from generations who came before us, but our conversations with Him are egocentric at best, non-existent at worst. They are passing pleasantries with an acquaintance.

When trouble ruptures our cleanly crafted lives, we grumble, we complain, and we question His goodness, not because we haven't seen His goodness, but because we don't consider it a reliable, repeatable characteristic. If only we had not been so silent toward Him. We give Israel a hard time for the doubts born from His silence, yet we submit ourselves to a much harder time

Chasing Rabbits

because our self-muzzled voice never reached His ears or touched His heart.

For the Israelites, as generations passed, the kindness of God was but a rumor, and while the glint of hope for a Savior's return remained, the potted meat filled their stomach and the roof over their head was the only safety they needed. The Egyptians understood a simple reality. If they slept well and ate well, they would toil well and withstand a greater deal of physical punishment. Now, wandering the desert, they felt the punishment but with empty stomachs. The songs of joy that once saturated the night air were replaced with communal gatherings to lament Moses's leadership and God's ability.

In their freedom, Israel had forgotten the weight of their oppressive yoke. Prior to the frogs and the locusts and the gnats came a significant amount of doubt. Moses came to them with a word from the Lord:

> "Moreover, I have heard the groaning of the people of Israel whom the Egyptians hold as slaves, and have remembered my covenant. Say therefore to the people of Israel, 'I am the Lord, and I will bring you out from under the burdens of the Egyptians, and I will deliver you from slavery to them, and I will redeem you with an outstretched arm and with great acts of judgment. I will take you to be my people and I will be your God, and you shall know that I am the Lord your God, who has brought you out from under the burdens of the Egyptians. I will bring you into the land that I swore to give to Abraham, to Isaac, and to Jacob. I will give it to you for a possession. I am the Lord.'" (Exodus 6:5–8)

Chasing Rabbits

But then comes verse 9, which is heartbreaking because it is so relatable, not in literal equality but in ramification: *"Moses spoke thus to the people of Israel,* **but they did not listen to Moses, because of their broken spirit and harsh slavery."**

Broken spirit and harsh slavery. The continual assault on their minds and their bodies ruptured their ability to think for themselves. The broken spirit resulted in hopelessness. Discouragement. Doubt. Fear. They were a fractured, failing people. They lost the ability to rise up, to fight, and to believe there was more. The promises of God were a pipe dream. This was their reality, and from their perspective, there was no changing it.

The broken body was injury to insult. They were physically assaulted, whipped, and abused. Many would die because of Egyptian strikes and lashes. They were so demoralized that even a word of hope and deliverance from God Himself through His servant would not be received. It cost too much to hope, and they simply could not part with even an ounce of physical or mental currency.

You may be able to relate. You may be reading this book and feeling completely broken in body and spirit. It hurts to hope. It is discouraging to dream. The Lord is saying, "Lift up your eyes, look to My promises. I will come for you and I will rescue you!"

It's almost satirical how we long for the back-and-forth conversations with a relational God and are rocked to our core when we hear nothing. Meanwhile, we utter only a few words to Him in the course of a day, week, month, or year, and expect instant intimacy at our point of suffering.

It would appear silence, much like money, has the latent capacity to be a blessing or a curse. It can be used to curate or crush. The difference between curation and crushing is the inten-

Chasing Rabbits

tion. Silence to receive versus silence to punish. Silence to learn versus silence to ignore.

The Sabbath was an invitation to a different kind of silence. It was not silent hopelessness; it was silent rest. They didn't have to think about bricks or farming or pleasing their taskmasters. They could just sit. Silence was welcomed, but if it was broken by their children's laughter, that was fine too.

Listening to God

Rabbits have the unique ability to catch sound from any direction simply by rotating an ear in that direction. Those ears can even move independently of each other. It's easy to determine whether a rabbit is listening to you simply by observing the position of their ears.

We sabotage the Sabbath when we ignore this lesson from the rabbit and fail to position our ears to hear from the Lord. Listening is a crucial spiritual skill refined in the beauty of the Sabbath, and it requires a primary communicator. The role of this primary communicator ebbs and flows. It is never static for long. Conversation always makes its way to the dinner table, water cooler, or comment box.

Proper communication cannot occur when more than one person with a different thought shares their thought at the same time. Communication must make way for the primary communicator to say their piece and then allow space for feedback. Hundreds of people talking at the same time is indecipherable and accomplishes nothing.

Inversely, however, hundreds of people can simultaneously sit in perfect silence. Only an omnipresent God could carry a

Chasing Rabbits

unique conversation with 7 billion people at the same time and not be confused or compromised in thought and deed.

The art of listening to God requires great discipline, as we need to lessen our thoughts of our own existence and focus on His thoughts of our existence. We may not find that very alluring. After all, we've thought long and hard about what God should do to ensure our happiness and our plan seems rock solid. It's not as if we've had certain plans fall through in the past. Or have we?

God's omnipresence positions Him to impart in the silence, but His omniscience is the icing on the cake. We reject patient listening because we are unaware of any plan other than our own that would fabricate the level of comfort and success we crave. There is only our way, with our conditions, our instruction, and our blessing. Silence is intrusive to those plans, and worse yet, if we do not know Jesus personally, silence is quite fearful. If our carefully formed plans are optimal, then what God would present must be dangerous. Missionary Frank Laubach put it this way: "Listening is far more important than giving Him your ideas."[2]

Yet, when we rotate our ear to God, we tap into the friendly yet formed ideas of our best future. We enter into the mysterious, uncertain, reassuring realm of relational perfection. We find clarity, not confusion. God's will is not discovered in our expressive prayers, but in our reluctant silence.

"Well then, when should I speak?" you may wonder. Perhaps that is the wrong question. God doesn't learn something when we speak, yet He encourages it. He knows every thought before we've formed the words to express it. Have you considered that you may talk less if you listen first? That He may give the answer before you ask the question? That praise, adoration, and exalta-

Chasing Rabbits

tion should be the most important components of a healthy prayer life?

Adoration followed by silence allows us to reconcile with our lofty ideals of self-importance and be humbled by His majesty. Once we are humbled, our requests no longer carry the same urgency because we understand how simple they are in light of an all-powerful God. It doesn't mean they should not be said. They should, as a form of partnership with what He is doing.

In our loquaciousness we silence God, which is a dreadful thing to do. Oswald Chambers once said, "To silence the voice of God is damnation in time!"[3] We violate the sacred space and time with our creator when we refuse to listen for His voice.

Perhaps the best course of action is to listen to God first. Then, with proper perspective, we make our requests known to Him. The only way we will ever experience "peace that transcends understanding" is if we are willing to kill our ideals for the sake of His.

Silence and Prayer

We can pray many types of prayers. There are prayers of petition (Ephesians 3:14–21; 1 Timothy 2:1–4), prayers of intercession (2 Corinthians 1:11; Philippians 1:19), prayers of deliverance (Psalm 3; Luke 22:39–42), prayers of adoration (Psalm 104:1–4; 1 Kings 8:22–24), and prayers of thanksgiving (Daniel 2:20–23; 1 Samuel 2:1–10). There are also prayers for spiritual warfare (2 Corinthians 10:3–5; Isaiah 54:17), prayers of faith (James 5:15; 1 John 5:14), prayers of consecration (Romans 12:1;

6:13), and prayers in the Holy Spirit (Jude 1:20–21; Romans 8:26).

Years ago, I sat in the office of a leader who had observed my prayer time. He, however, did not critique my prayer; he critiqued my silence. How anyone could feel qualified to critique someone's conversation with God is beyond me, but I remember leaving that meeting feeling quite frustrated. My silence was filled with introspection, meditating on Scripture, and concentrated listening because I needed to hear from God each day. I knew what was on my checklist to accomplish, but I needed to hear from Holy Spirit, and talking over Him would not do.

Please don't misunderstand. This is not aggression toward those who pray roaring prayers of great volume. I'm convinced praying loudly causes the enemy to tremble. Something always happens when we pray. The enemy cannot read our minds, as he is not all-knowing, but he can hear our decrees, our declarations, and our kingdom intervention against what he is doing in the spiritual realm. Praying aloud also models prayer for those who are just now dipping their toes in the water of communion with God. I once heard it said that we learn how to pray by being around people who pray. Audible prayers are encouraging and lift our faith.

"Didn't Jesus condemn the religious leaders for praying aloud for all to hear?" you may ask. Yes, but this was not a matter of content or volume. It was a matter of motive. If a person intends to be noticed, no amount of amplification will reach the Father. Passionate prayer is not about volume; it's about conviction. Conviction may drive our voice louder and louder as we desperately seek His throne, but make no mistake, He also hears the sigh, and He is even found in the whisper (1 Kings 19:11–13).

We exist in a culture where the squeaky wheel gets not the oil, but a brand-new bike. I wonder if the Lord is pleased with those who superficially draw attention to themselves, pretending to draw attention to God? Superfluous speech may make one sound quite spiritual, but our goal should be to know Him and be known by Him, to point every person to the cross so they can cast their gaze upon His signature and not our social media. An unhealthy mixture of insecurity and ambition will beg for recognition, but any home built on recognition not initiated by the Father will not withstand the huffing and puffing of the big bad wolf (in this case, Satan).

In his book *The Signature of Jesus: The Call to a Life Marked by Holy Passion and Relentless Faith*, Brennan Manning writes,

> If indeed we lived a life in imitation of his, our witness would be irresistible. If we dared to live beyond our self-concern; if we refused to shrink from being vulnerable; if we took nothing but a compassionate attitude toward the world; if we were a counterculture to our nation's lunatic lust for pride of place, power, and possessions; if we preferred to be faithful rather than successful, the walls of indifference to Jesus Christ would crumble. A handful of us could be ignored by society; but hundreds, thousands, millions of such servants would overwhelm the world. Christians filled with the authenticity, commitment, and generosity of Jesus would be the most spectacular sign in the history of the human race. The call of Jesus is revolutionary. If we implemented it, we would change the world in a few months.[4]

Chasing Rabbits

Such a revelation is cultivated in silence, not in the ambition's commotion. We cannot possibly respond to God's voice if we are unable to discern it from the world's.

Mother Teresa once commented, "In the silence of the heart God speaks. If you face God in prayer and silence, God will speak to you. Then you will know that you are nothing. It is only when you realize your nothingness, your emptiness, that God can fill you with Himself. Souls of prayer are souls of great silence."[5]

The psalmist declared, "For God alone, O my soul, wait in silence, for my hope is from him" (Psalm 62:5). And Moses declared, "The Lord will fight for you, and you have only to be silent" (Exodus 14:14).

An omniscient God desires both intense intercession and concentrated silence. The Sabbath is a gift where we can focus on silence and nothing else. Every other day of the week we may seek to hear His voice for direction and accomplishment, but what would happen if we committed our Sabbath to spending time with Him as a child would their father at an amusement park? What if the Sabbath became a practice of sacred conversation where one listens before speaking, not for advancement but for familiarity and friendship? We would certainly learn to long for silence with expectation, not disappointment. Silence would not be a punishment, but an appetizer.

Even King David struggled with silence (Psalm 13:1–2), but one could argue he should have known better. This is the man who spent countless hours by himself tending to sheep. Perhaps his new elevated position caused him to forget the still, quiet moments in the pasture. Silence is often transformed into emotion. If we are not akin to the practice of silence, we will panic when it comes.

Chasing Rabbits

The Sabbath prepares us for the moments when we are not yet prepared for His instruction. When we can exist in the silence of the Sabbath, we can enjoy His presence before receiving His provision. Silence enables us to "lean not on our own understanding" (Proverbs 3:5) by ceasing to offer God our opinion on what He should do and why He should do it, casting our cares on Him without an instruction manual.

In Psalm 62:1, David says, *"For God alone, my soul waits in silence; from him comes my salvation."*

Have you ever asked a tough question, or perhaps an awkward one, only to be greeted with extended silence? The temptation is to fill the void. To say something. Anything. But if you let the question linger, or the statement sit still, inevitably the other person will speak. They will break the silence because it is easier to stammer through an answer than to sit in uncertainty.

God is not like us and He is not subject to our whims or manipulations, but He is a good Father. Even imperfect fathers answer their children. Maybe you need to just ask the question and be silent. Wait for Him to fill the void with something meaningful, not a haphazard attempt to escape the discomfort.

Don't make the silent moments of your Sabbath awkward. Allow them to be transcendent.

Awe-Induced Silence

Michael Jordan was my childhood hero. I had more than ten Jordan posters covering my bedroom walls. Like many children my age, I wanted to be like Mike. Although short, not particularly fast, and not naturally athletic, I played basketball daily. Two to three hours a day were devoted to my craft. I never longed to be like any other player but Mike. I was even a member of the Air Jordan Flight Club, and my first expensive pair of shoes were the Air Jordan VIs. I knew every stat, watched every game I could, and celebrated every championship like it was my own.

The first time I saw Michael Jordan in person, I was in Las Vegas for a vacation with some close friends. Jordan was in town for his annual basketball camp and was staying at the same hotel as my friends and me. We were on high alert, always surveying the grounds for a glimpse of His Airness. On our second day in Vegas, as we exited an elevator near the hotel casino, my friend Jeff stopped abruptly in front of me. His jaw dropped, and he stood frozen, utterly silent. His head turned slowly and mine followed.

There he was. Michael Jordan, walking right by us! We were awestruck and couldn't mumble a single word. All we could do was stand there and stare at this man, who was so much taller than we had imagined, with his entourage of a dozen people following closely behind. We didn't budge. We just stood there and watched him walk by. Speechless.

Later, a friend asked me why I didn't approach him for an autograph or a conversation. It wasn't his personal security or his collection of sycophants that deterred me. I simply didn't want to meet him. I was sure I'd be disappointed or rejected. He was clearly not approachable, and after watching a recent documentary on him, I'm happy with my decision not to offer my childhood balloon to be popped. This was my reaction to a flawed, faulty person who never did anything for me. While I enjoy being a fan, he never won awards or championships for me. Yet I stood in awe as he passed by.

Chasing Rabbits

Why are we not in even greater awe of our Lord who, while we were yet sinners, died for us (see Romans 5:8)? Why are we not in awe of the One who created the stars in the skies and holds the entire world in His hands? Why do we take for granted His majesty and treat Him as less than a prolific basketball player?

It's only in knowing God, resting in His presence, feasting at His table, that our awe is restored. Only then can we echo the apostle Paul, "Oh, the depth of the riches and wisdom and knowledge of God! How unreachable are his judgments and how inscrutable his ways" (Romans 11:33).

Perhaps we become so accustomed to His goodness that we've lost track of His holiness.

Author and Theologian Ralph Enlow elaborates,

> In the Gospels and Acts, the Greek phobos, the common word for fear, is occasionally translated "awe," or "filled with awe." It describes people's reaction to astonishing works of God such as Jesus's demonstration of authority to forgive sins (see Luke 5:26), the raising of the widow's son (see Luke 7:16), or the outpouring of the Holy Spirit in the early church (see Acts 2:43).
>
> When humans are confronted with God's awesome presence, our inevitable response is to quiver and cower. In fact, the Bible never records a direct personal encounter with God in which the individual was not visibly shaken by God's awesomeness. When God appeared to Moses in the burning bush, Moses hid his face and trembled (Exodus 3:6). When Isaiah saw the Lord in his glory and majesty, he cried, "Woe is me, for I am ruined!" (Isaiah 6:5 NASB 1995). When the risen

Christ appeared to Saul the persecutor on the Damascus road, Saul prostrated himself in fear and trembling (Acts 9:3). The Bible emphasizes, however, that genuine awe is primarily a disposition rather than merely an emotional state.

God's person and His works of creation, providence, redemption, and judgment are astounding and demand both sober contemplation and humble submission. God's people are commanded to show proper regard for His power and dominion—His absolute authority to rule (see Job 25:2; Jeremiah 33:9) and His power to perform what He will (see Deuteronomy 4:34; 34:12; 1 Samuel 12:18; Habakkuk 3:2). On the other hand, the Bible makes it clear that there will come a day when those who refuse to acknowledge God's awesomeness will tremble and wail before His vengeful presence and His righteous judgment (Jeremiah 2:19; Zephaniah 2:11).[6]

We need not reserve our awe of God for another moment in time. The Sabbath is a weekly opportunity to be enamored by him again.

Silence as God's Answer

While awe and silence may go hand in hand, I'd argue that silence is not God's intention. He desires a daily encounter with us. "What do I do when He is silent?" you may ask. "If He desperately wants to speak to us, why are there seasons when we can't hear Him?"

What if silence is His answer? What if we are not capable of receiving the bigness of His answer, so silence is the only appropriate response?

Chasing Rabbits

Perhaps this is a question of character, not conversation. God is not one to cast pearls before swine. We must ask ourselves if we can effectively steward an answer larger than our resources or our imagination. Do we trust the foundation of intimacy we've laid with Him?

When we find ourselves in a season of silence, the answer is simple. Not easy, but simple. Focus on His written Word. It is living and active (Hebrews 4:12), always present tense. The person who bellyaches over His silence is likely among those who seldomly read His Word. The person who has dined on His Word has found the psalmist's praise to be true: "How sweet are your words to my taste, sweeter than honey to my mouth!" (Psalm 119:103).

I don't need to hear from my parents every day to know they love me, are praying for me, and are always for me. They trust that they have raised me well (see Proverbs 22:6), and they trust in the veracity of their instruction. When I was a child, they gave me the tools to live a righteous, holy life. I must simply walk it out. God has given us all we need, and in times of silence, we must simply walk out His Word. David declared, "Blessed are those whose way is blameless, who walk in the law of the Lord!" (Psalm 119:1). When God is silent, just keep walking, day and night, in His Word.

If only He recommended one day a week to study His Word and listen for His voice (sarcasm intended).

Perhaps God has not fulfilled what He spoke to you last. Much like the Israelites who had to wait 430 years for their liberation, and the 400 silent years of the intertestamental period between the last words of the Prophets in the Old Testament to the coming of Jesus the Messiah, sometimes we just have to wait.

Chasing Rabbits

In the meantime, His Word is a lamp to our feet and a light to our path (Psalm 119:105). Trust His Word until you hear His voice.

Silence is graceful. It is a spiritual blank page, full of promise to the prolific artist or verbose writer. The silence of the Sabbath chips away the barnacles of indifference from our hearts, and we may find ourselves weeping in His presence, yet not hear a single word from Him.

We're never sure when He will call or what He may ask of us. He may arouse us from our sleep or interrupt us midday. Reclaim the beauty found in the silent days of the Sabbath. Talking too much often has less to do with His plans and more to do with our impatience with the space between.

And don't worry. Chances are, He won't make you wait 430 years.

THE PROBLEM OF PRIDE

CHAPTER FOUR

"In general, pride is at the bottom of all great mistakes!"
– John Ruskin

It's a story we've all probably heard at one time or another. A Hare was making fun of the Tortoise for being so slow. "Do you ever get anywhere?" he asked with a mocking laugh.

"Yes," replied the Tortoise, "and I get there sooner than you think. I'll run you a race and prove it."

The Hare was much amused by the idea of running a race with the Tortoise, but for the fun of the thing, he agreed. So the Fox, who had consented to act as judge, marked the distance and started the runners off.

The Hare was soon far out of sight, and to make the Tortoise feel very deeply how ridiculous it was for him to try a race with a Hare, he lay down beside the course to take a nap until the Tortoise should catch up. The Tortoise, meanwhile, kept going slowly but steadily, and, after a time, passed the place where the Hare was sleeping. But the Hare slept on very peacefully—and when at last he did wake up, the Tortoise was near the goal. The Hare now ran his swiftest, but he could not overtake the Tortoise in time.

The Tortoise and the Hare is a fascinating story told a hundred different ways to a million different kids. Aesop wisely leaves the interpretation and application of the story to the reader. Perhaps it's about staying consistent amid adversity. Maybe it's a David-and-Goliath story where the underdog wins the battle against all odds. Or maybe it's a fable about the value of a slow, methodical approach to the advancement of the mission versus the flash-in-the-pan moments of temporary success.

Those are all great and applicable interpretations, but I think the truth runs much deeper. I think it's about pride and the catastrophic burden of pain it dispenses so freely.

I believe the Tortoise knew the outcome of the race long before it was even suggested. I believe he discerned the character of the Hare amid the mockery and issued an intelligent challenge, not based on the physical imbalance but on the indecorum of the Hare. The cottontail had his laugh at the expense of the torpid Tortoise, poking and prodding the terrapin to get a rise, but his pride and arrogance produced a race that should never have been, and yielded a result the Hare would never live down. No doubt, the Hare would have wanted an immediate rematch to redeem his shame, much like the boxer who is upset by a no-name fighter and immediately demands a rematch to save face. It's Apollo and Rocky in fable form. The Tortoise won the day, and there was nothing the Hare could do but sit in his frustration, rage, and overflowing regret.

I envision a gang of tortoises hoisting the victor on their shoulders and slowly, ever so slowly, carrying him over the horizon into the sunset, as to mock the woebegone rabbit standing idly by. Salt in the proverbial wound.

Then came the onslaught of destructive thoughts, wave after wave, as if the Hare was floating adrift in a violent ocean. "I'll never live this down. I'm a disgrace. Why did I take a nap? If only I could do this over, I wouldn't make the same mistake. All I need is one more chance! Why did I pick on that tortoise to begin with? What's wrong with me? Who would do such a stupid thing? I would. I deserve everything I'm getting. I'm a poor excuse for a rabbit. I lost a race to a turtle! I can never face my friends or family again. I'm so stupid, stupid, stupid."

Chances are, the Hare didn't sleep much that night. He sadistically replayed his failure over and over again. Not just his failure, but also the Tortoise's victory. The shouts of joy. The look of exhilaration on the terrapins' faces while his world came crashing down. It was almost too much.

The next morning, the Hare awakened thinking perhaps it was just a nightmare, only to see the video, with commentary, in his social media feed. He read the comments. One should never read the comments. Why absorb criticism from someone you wouldn't go to for advice?

Yet, he read them. Every comment. Every. Single. One.

We've all visited the tropical island of regret. At the crest of its shores stands an impressive all-inclusive resort where the only cost to stay at such a lavish establishment is an unhealthy, demonstrably prideful heart.

The Issue of Pride

If ever a sin were to rob the Sabbath of its strength, it would be pride. The prideful person overestimates the plausible with little consideration for what lies dormant. Just like the Hare who thought more of himself than he ought to, so does the haughty person as they disregard God's commands. Pride causes us to think we can do it alone. If we convince ourselves that we don't need God to be healthy and successful, we will also convince ourselves that we don't need to obey God's demands.

And if we need not obey His commands, then we are free to feed our passion for degradation, tossing our flesh more and more choice foods until our spirit is starved and no longer perceives the conviction necessary for righteousness and holiness. Scripture repetitively warns of the disastrous consequences of pride, yet we hear very few sermons, and even fewer warnings, of its ruinous ways.

When pride comes, disgrace follows (Proverbs 11:2). What is disgrace? A reversal of God's favor. Disregarding the Sabbath on account of self-reliant ambition will not end well. Ironically, the pride that would keep us from resting on the Sabbath is actually robbing us of the very vitality and favor that would make us great. As we gaze upon Holy Spirit with an unrestricted stare, humbling ourselves in the shadow of His omniscience and being content with just a glimpse of His glory, He bestows the very thing our pride has longed for.

What did the Hare long for? Not what he should have. The Hare longed to be treasured for his speed and wit, so he ostentatiously paraded both. He was confident enough in himself to brazenly want what he did not have, and he wanted it all. He wanted the recognition. He wanted the celebration. He wanted the TV commercials and the big house and the nice car and the private jet. He wanted the large bank account and the book deals. He wanted it all, and somehow what he felt stood in his way—the Tortoise—was not what was in his way at all.

A Biblical Precedent

There is a biblical precedent for what occurred with the Tortoise and the Hare. Solomon, the widely accepted writer of Ecclesiastes, notes,

> I have seen something else under the sun:
> The race is not to the swift
> or the battle to the strong,
> nor does food come to the wise
> or wealth to the brilliant

or favor to the learned;
but time and chance happen to them all. (9:11 NIV)

No one stays on top forever. Age and calamity exist outside our control. We may feel we've succeeded thus far, not honoring the Sabbath. We may believe our successes have entitled us to a cosmic pass. Perhaps God is so impressed with our accomplishments, we are now exempt from this specific command. Pride provides comfort in disobedience, safety in rebellion. It ensures us we'll be okay as we walk blindfolded toward the cliff's edge.

Time and chance. They happen to us all. Yet we are called to steward our time honorably (Ephesians 5:15-16). While we cannot speed up or slow down time (looking at my four-year-old, I wish I could!), we can establish rhythms that allow us to maximize what is allotted us. Time may happen to us, in that we cannot prevent the progression of age, but we can also happen to time. In fact, we are commanded to "happen to" time. All the days ordained for us were written in His book before one of them came to be, yet within the brackets of allotted time exists a humble palace where pride is starved of its strength and synergistic surrender multiplies kingdom ambition.

The Hare should have longed for wisdom as passionately as he longed for recognition, yet it was the very trait our prideful antagonist failed to attain. The rabbit knew he was fast, but he lacked the right application of knowledge. Wisdom.

Pride resulted in Lucifer being cast down from heaven. Pride forces us to say yes when we should say no. And pride causes us to think we can do more working seven days on our own than working six days with God.

When we play the composition of life in the key of pride, our opus becomes one of shame. Comparison, perfection, insecurity, and fear are our major chords. We can't stomach the thought of failure, so we manipulate, demean, and demonstrably pout in lieu of resting in His presence.

If only we would come to the flagrant revelation that we are nothing outside of Him—that we can do nothing outside of Him. Compared to His precious, exquisite glory, every trophy we present means nothing. Less than nothing. He is our portion. He is our all in all. He is our reward, our prize, our righteous compensation. He is holy. He is worthy. He is everything we need and more. Better is one day in His courts than a thousand elsewhere (Psalm 84:10), yet we can simplify even that. Better one day out of seven. One day, focused on Him, listening to Him, enjoying rest in Him. One day.

Pride also inflates the misconception that we provide for ourselves. Humanity has struggled with this for thousands of years. God was very clear to His people about where their strength and supply came from, yet there was always a yearning for self-sufficiency.

> When you have eaten and are satisfied, praise the Lord your God for the good land he has given you. Be careful that you do not forget the Lord your God, failing to observe his commands, his laws and his decrees that I am giving you this day. Otherwise, when you eat and are satisfied, when you build fine houses and settle down, and when your herds and flocks grow large and your silver and gold increase and all you have is multiplied, then your heart will become proud and you will forget the Lord your God, who brought you out of Egypt, out of the

land of slavery. He led you through the vast and dreadful wilderness, that thirsty and waterless land, with its venomous snakes and scorpions. He brought you water out of hard rock. He gave you manna to eat in the wilderness, something your ancestors had never known, to humble and test you so that in the end it might go well with you. You may say to yourself, "My power and the strength of my hands have produced this wealth for me." But remember the Lord your God, for it is he who gives you the ability to produce wealth, and so confirms his covenant, which he swore to your ancestors, as it is today. (Deuteronomy 8:10–18 NIV)

We overcomplicate God's simple requests. Give thanks to God, from whom our blessings flow. Observe His commands (hello, Sabbath). If we don't, our successes will lead to pride and will induce spiritual amnesia as well as mystical myopia. We'll forget Him and we'll only see what is directly in front of us: our hands, our work, our successes, and our effort. We may say we are responsible for our wealth and provision. We may say it was by the sweat of our brow we found success. We may say our achievements are self-made.

But remember, the Lord is of the beginning. Our successes are fleeting, and our wealth is temporal, but He never lacks. When we give something away, we no longer have that thing, but not God. When He gives, it does not affect His cosmic accounts in the least. He is the God of abundance. He is the God who longs to give and can do so without paucity. If we give everything away, we are left with nothing but a memory, but it's impossible for Him to give everything away, as every created thing comes from Him. Creation was not a moment for Him. It is constant. Newness is in His nature. He honors and tends to what was already given or created (stewardship), and He prepares us for what will come. God is a present-tense historical futurist.

In His kindness, He established a day when our future planning could come to a halt and we could loaf around in His presence without recourse. He stands outside of time, yet created a time we should honor. He does not need to slow down for us. Instead, He slows down time for us, and slows us down for time. He pauses the things we hold no sway over and calls us to come, sit, and dine with Him. He beckons us to open our souls to a divine rest we cannot earn, only receive.

When pride barges in and attempts to get its way, we need only look at the cross and its embodied humility. Oh, that rugged cross, where Jesus extended an invitation to come, not to experience physical torture, but to find something much deeper and more resounding. He invited us to find freedom through Him. Freedom from our sin-stained souls, freedom from inflated egos and narcissistic ambitions, freedom from dysfunctional relationships and depraved thought. Freedom from pointless striving and the pursuit of mechanical rabbits. It is the Sabbath, instituted at creation and reiterated through Christ, where we can set aside what we want for what we need.

We want more, we need less. He wants more, we give less. In Christ, less is more and more becomes less. As we give Him more, the value of the attainable decreases and the benefit of the discarnate is multiplied. The kingdom of God is upside down. Creation is structured to be reliant on God, not man. We are only to be stewards of what is sacredly subservient. In this way, the impossible becomes normal. Six days of work produces eight days of results, and seven days of work produces six days of results. Pretension will always yield less than submission.

Chasing Rabbits

Pride Leads to Disobedience

The Old Testament story of King Asa can also be our story, both the good and the bad. A story of both pride and submission, it is an exhortation and a warning. Asa's reign had started off as it should. He "did what was right in the eye of the Lord" (2 Chronicles 14:2). He tore down the altars erected to foreign gods, and he led as leaders should—by example. He turned Judah's attention back to the Holy One in word, deed, and law, and committed to completely rely on the Lord. His reliance brought great reward.

Even when attacked by a million-man Ethiopian army, he did not waiver. "And Asa cried to the Lord his God, 'O Lord, there is none like you to help, between the mighty and the weak. Help us, O Lord our God, for we rely on you, and in your name we have come against the multitude. O Lord, you are our God; let no man prevail against you'" (v. 11). The Lord answered and routed the army. None were left, because when the Lord does a thing, He does it completely.

This further emboldened Asa's commitment to God. He passed sweeping religious reforms, even removing his own mother from her queenship because she made a "detestable image for Asherah." The Lord acknowledged his efforts and positioned him for success. Then,

> The Spirit of God came upon Azariah the son of Oded, and he went out to meet Asa and said to him, "Here me, Asa, and all Judah and Benjamin: the Lord is with you while you are with him. If you seek him, he will be found by you, but if you forsake him, he will forsake you. For a long time Israel was

Chasing Rabbits

without the true God, and without a teaching priest and without law, but when in their distress they turned to the Lord, the God of Israel, and sought him, he was found by them. . . . Do not let your hands be weak, for your work shall be rewarded." (2 Chronicles 15:1–7)

The promise is sound and the source is impeccable, yet in 2 Chronicles 16, King Asa did a foolish thing. Bashah, King of Israel, tried to keep any resources from going in or out of Judah. He was going to starve them out, deplete their resources, frustrate the people, and ultimately weaken Judah to the extent that they either waived a white flag or fought with a minimal chance of success. Bashah had aligned with others, and Asa did not have the military might to compete.

You may wonder why Asa didn't go back to that impeccable source. You may ask how, with such a clear prophetic word and the Lord's support, he would ever waiver and turn to other hands to lift his burden. Scripture doesn't say why Asa drifted. Perhaps he became lethargic in his pursuit of righteousness. Maybe he was swayed by surrounding himself with the wrong people. Either way, his faith faltered. He turned to the king of Syria and formed an alliance that seemed to go against the covenant God had made with Asa, and the result was heartbreaking:

> At that time Hanani the seer came to Asa king of Judah and said to him, "Because you relied on the king of Syria, and did not rely on the Lord your God, the army of the king of Syria has escaped you. Were not the Ethiopians and the Libyans a huge army with very many chariots and horsemen? Yet because you relied on the Lord, he gave them into your hand. For the eyes of the Lord run to and fro throughout the whole

earth, to give strong support to those whose heart is blameless toward him. You have done foolishly in this, for from now on you will have wars." Then Asa was angry with the seer and put him in the stocks in prison, for he was in a rage with him because of this. And Asa inflicted cruelties upon some of the people at the same time. (2 Chronicles 16:7–10)

Asa trusted in others for provision and protection even though God had proven Himself faithful time and time again. Asa's reaction was symbolic of a heart that had turned from the Lord. I believe the wars were not just external. They were also formed in his heart and psyche, and executed with passion on his own people. Somehow Asa simultaneously thought highly of himself but had a low opinion of God. Only pride can dismember a relationship so quickly.

The Lord is constantly looking for people whose hearts are blameless toward Him so as to provide "strong support," and all He asks is that we trust Him and obey His commands.

Theologian Martin Selman expounds on Asa's journey:

> Asa's last five years, recounted in chapter 16, completely reverse the pattern of the rest of his life, a decline that is all the more unexpected in that it seems to have started from an act of unprovoked hostility (v. 1). From that point on, however, Asa seemed determined to go his own way, and he followed his initial rejection of God's help (vv. 2–3) by persecuting a prophet (v. 10), oppressing his people (v. 10), and neglecting God (v. 12). A pattern therefore developed, which, though it may have begun by accident, became a series of conscious decisions.[1]

Chasing Rabbits

He also adds,

> The theme of the chapter is a negative version of chapters 14–15, turning from faith and trust to unbelief. Asa relied on human beings rather than God (vv. 6–7; cf. 14:11), and failed to seek God as he had done previously (v. 12).[2]

And so we prove Proverbs 16:18: "Pride goes before destruction, and a haughty spirit before a fall." Consider the following verses as well.

- "If anyone thinks he is something, when he is nothing, he deceives himself" (Galatians 6:3).
- "One's pride will bring him low, but he who is lowly in spirit will obtain honor" (Proverbs 29:23).
- "The fear of the Lord is hatred of evil. Pride and arrogance and the way of evil and perverted speech I hate" (Proverbs 8:13).
- "But he gives more grace. Therefore it says, 'God opposes the proud, but gives grace to the humble'" (James 4:6).
- "Everyone who is arrogant in heart is an abomination to the Lord; be assured, he will not go unpunished" (Proverbs 16:5).

Yeah, the Bible has a lot to say about pride, and its implications are numerous when we ignore the Sabbath—but many still don't see the need to rest. They consider themselves strong, capable, and efficient. Maybe they believe their past successes have offered some sort of carnal roadmap toward accomplishment. Maybe they relish in the celebration of hurry. Whatever reasoning they have for not needing the Sabbath, it is wrong, and they will never be as effective as they could be by learning how to submit their plans to His grace and allow Him to direct their steps.

Reclaiming the beauty of the Sabbath means embracing the revelation that our speed doesn't matter in the race of obedience. If we're not careful to obey, we'll find ourselves burned out, asleep under a tree, pride in hand, while God uses someone less qualified but fiercely more obedient to cross the finish line with adulation.

Chasing Rabbits

WAIT

CHAPTER FIVE

"We must let go of the life we have planned, so as to accept the one that is waiting for us" - Joseph Campbell

"Shhhh . . . I'm hunting wabbit."

Poor Elmer Fudd. He wanted a win so badly. He had become a hunter. Hunters are active, even in the stillness. Whether sitting in a blind or cautiously moving through the woods with a finger on the trigger, hunters are always engaged. They understand they may only have a moment. A blink, a wrong step, a shift in the wind, and their prey may be gone before they ever lift their weapon.

I like to imagine Elmer was a successful hunter before meeting Bugs Bunny. He may have had a fantastic two-bedroom log cabin with multiple trophies donning the walls. Maybe he had a moose head over his fireplace and a twelve-point buck over his bed. Perhaps he was even into taxidermy. He was good at hunting; he just wasn't good at hunting Bugs Bunny.

The problem with Elmer was that he always acted too soon. He was so eager to catch that "wascally wabbit" that he never took time to set a convincing trap. His impatience produced half-cocked schemes that were easy to sniff out. If only he had relied on the same patience that produced success with the moose and the deer.

The Inability to Wait

Like Elmer, we are impatient people. As a result, the Sabbath feels like spiritual sandpaper to us. Hunters understand active waiting. They realize they may have to sit in a tree for long hours, fully engaged in what is happening around them. Silent, listening, alerting all their senses for a chance to catch what they're after. Fisherman understand the principle of active waiting as well. They know they may sit in a boat for five hours and

Chasing Rabbits

come home with nothing, yet feel fulfilled. They are recharged in the waiting.

Humans are much better with evaluation than expectation. The beauty of the Sabbath is found in the waiting, because in the waiting God is still working. Waiting activates our faith, which produces results through His effort, not ours. Waiting nurtures the charm of expectation.

One thing that plays a significant role in our inability to wait is tiredness. According to the CDC, we need seven to nine hours of sleep to be effective, yet only 35.2 percent of all U.S. adults report getting less than seven hours of sleep per night.[1] Almost half say they feel sleepy during the day between three and seven days per week.[2]

It's hard to wait when we're exhausted. We've all been there. Despite our best intentions, the moment that we set aside time to wait on the Lord, our eyelids collapse on themselves and we awaken thirty minutes later, slightly refreshed but frustrated. We let another spiritual moment slip away. We kick ourselves and swear we'll do better next time.

It's not hard to sympathize with disciples Peter, James, and John, who Jesus took into the garden of Gethsemane for a time of intense prayer, watching, and waiting (Matthew 26:36–46). It didn't matter how important the moment was; they were exhausted, unable to stay awake with Jesus whose "soul was overwhelmed with sorrow to the point of death" (v. 38 NIV).

Jesus asked them to remain alert, stay awake, and be watchful. He could trust them, right? They were His big three! Peter, James, and John were there at the transfiguration (Matthew 17:1–13), so the magnitude of Christ's mission was not wasted on them. They were thick as thieves, and surely if anyone was going to have Jesus's back it would be them, right? Peter had just pledged his faithfulness, even until death (Matthew 26:35), so waiting on Jesus was going to be a breeze.

But it's so hard to find spiritual strength in physical weariness.

Three times Jesus returned to the disciples, and each time He found them sleeping. Three times Jesus acknowledged their weak flesh but exhorted them to do better nonetheless. The first exhortation was to remain, stay awake, and be watchful. The second exhortation was similar, but with some added emphasis and potential ramifications: Be awake, alert, and watchful, but also pray so you don't fall into temptation. It's almost as if Jesus was saying, "I understand, you have great intentions, but your flesh has taken the lead and your spirit has taken a back seat. If your flesh continues to dictates your choices, you'll succumb to temptation and forfeit your promise." The third time Jesus saw them, He said nothing. He just returned to praying. I can't imagine how hopeless He felt in that moment, how disappointed.

The fourth time Jesus saw them, He was already moving on. "Get up, you can rest later. You were unable to stay and watch, and now here they come." I don't know about you, but I'd be ticked off, sarcastic, and passive-aggressive. "Hey, I'm good, thanks. Just make sure you get a little shut-eye while I am tortured, verbally assaulted, and carry the sins of all humanity for all time upon my frame. By all means, I want you to be rested when you betray me."

Three times Peter denied Christ. The same Peter who slept on Jesus in the garden of Gethsemane also slept on Jesus after He was captured. The failure in the latter was likely linked to the failure in the former. James and John were not mentioned in the

Chasing Rabbits

Matthew passage, which instead emphasizes Peter's botched reliability and faithfulness, both in the present and future.

Three times the disciples fell asleep, three times Jesus prayed that the cup would be taken from Him, and three times Peter would betray Him. In this dark season, after all he'd done for them, Jesus experienced three acts of betrayal: the disciples inability to stay awake, Judas's kiss, and Peter's denial.

Much like the number seven, the number three also carries the symbolism of "completeness." There are three in the Trinity, Paul went on three primary missionary journeys, there are three woes of judgment, and Jesus rose on the third day, to name just a few instances of its use. The number three matters. It ushers in a measure of finality and fruitfulness.

Would the outcome have been different had the disciples stayed awake? Hard to say, but likely not. These things had to happen. Jesus was placed on the cross at the third hour of the day, there were three hours of darkness while Jesus was on the cross, and He rose again on the third day. Our God is not a God of half-measures. He brings all things to completeness. Our disregard for His commands empowers our flesh to rule over our spirit, and in doing so we hijack the very things that would position us for success.

Waiting and the Sabbath

Rest is paramount to our progress. The Sabbath invites us to wait, once again—to answer the call Peter, James, and John so eluded. Be alert, be awake, and be watchful. Resting becomes cyclical. We rest on the Sabbath to be alert to His voice, prepared to hear and apply whatever He would choose to impart. Yet, we must rest in order to wait, so we do not fall asleep and succumb to temptation. The spirit is willing, but the flesh is weak (Matthew 26:41), so we must discipline our flesh and yet give it rest (Sabbath). The spirit must never occupy a secondary role to our flesh. Proper order, and proper rest, will ensure we are available when He calls.

With this in mind, is it possible that God does not use some people because they are not good stewards of the Sabbath? After all, if He can't trust us to obey His command to rest, and He knows because of our lack of discipline we will succumb to temptation, why would He give us more responsibility, regardless of how willing our flesh may be?

We prefer to link the concept of weak flesh to some grievous, repulsive sin. But is not disobedience to His commands just that? Grievous and repulsive? Would not a command that is referenced over 170 times in the Bible be worth our attention? Do we think He would call it holy for His benefit and not ours? To dishonor the Sabbath is to neglect our frame and our future. Before we feel the need to prove He can trust us with leadership, wealth, success, or influence, perhaps we should show Him He can trust us just with ourselves, with our sacred time with Him, and with caring for our temporary temple.

Waiting is not without a treasured promise. The prophet Isaiah said it this way: "But they who wait for the Lord shall renew their strength; they shall mount up with wings like eagles; they shall run and not be weary; they shall walk and not faint" (Isaiah 40:3). The number three appears here as well. There are three benefits to waiting on the Lord: renewed strength, re-engaged purpose, and reward. These flow from our waiting. The

Chasing Rabbits

tenderness of God is made evident in the Sabbath. He is essentially commanding us to be renewed, engaged, and rewarded.

But before we get to the flying and walking and running, we must backtrack to the magnificent setup found in Isaiah 40:28–30:

> Have you not known? Have you not heard?
> The Lord is the everlasting God,
>   the Creator of the ends of the earth.
> He does not faint or grow weary;
>   his understanding is unsearchable.
> He gives power to the faint,
>   and to him who has no might he increases strength.
> Even youths shall faint and be weary,
>   and young men shall fall exhausted.

The tension found in God's omnipotence is both a comfort and a curiosity. He has always been, He will always be, and it is literally impossible to search out the fullness of His being. We will never understand the immeasurable beauty, wisdom, and glory of God. What we can be sure of is that He is incapable of losing step, tripping up, or growing weary. On the contrary, He pulls out of His inexhaustible supply a measure of power to the limited man or woman who so desperately needs it, without subtracting from His power at all.

No human is exempt from fatigue, whether physical, mental, spiritual, or emotional. But then comes the good news as we revisit Isaiah 40:31. It's the kind of news that will make a defeated man shout for joy. Isaiah 40:28 delivers the good news from God's perspective, and verse 31 delivers the good news from our

Chasing Rabbits

perspective, and it starts with a simple but glorious conjunction—*but*.

"But those who wait on the Lord . . ." It doesn't matter who you are, how tired you've become, or how hopeless things may seem. If you wait on the Lord, miracles begin to happen. Things that once lay dormant are awakened. His promise will activate according to your faith and obedience and you'll begin to breathe again.

- Your family may be a mess, but if you wait on the Lord . . .
- Your ministry may be flailing, but if you wait on the Lord . . .
- Your work may be a constant fight, but if you wait on the Lord . . .

When your striving becomes dormant in His presence, He finds a vessel to breathe renewed life into.

Artificial Strength

America consumes an estimated 146 *billion* cups of coffee per year. That's 400 *million* cups of coffee every single day. Now, I love coffee. If you love Jesus, you probably do too. I love the taste, and I love the energy it gives. Seldom do I go a day without a cup . . . or two . . . or three. Yet for all the joy coffee brings me, I understand its nature. It is artificial, temporary strength. It has addictive qualities proved by the piercing headache I suffer when I fast and give it up for a few days.

Caffeine is fabricated strength. For many, it's a costly fix to bad habits (pot, meet kettle). When adversity comes, we often turn to controllable substances. I can control how many cups of coffee I consume to stay awake and alert for the tasks at hand. Even now, at 10:44 p.m. as I write this chapter, I wish I had a cup of coffee next to me.

Conversely, the amount of strength God gives is not within our control. We do not govern what He gives; we control what we receive. If we feel a consumable like coffee is enough to sustain us physically and that physical sustainability functions independently of spiritual vitality, we may be quick to substitute unremitting renewed strength with roasted rejuvenation.

God doesn't just renew our physical bodies. He also renews a right spirit. The mudslinging of this world can force the greatest of men to cry out, "Unclean!" When sin has blackened the best parts of us, we can still stand before Him and cry David's prayer, "Create in me a clean spirit, O God, and renew a right spirit within me" (Psalm 51:10).

If you think spiritual renewal and physical renewal aren't intricately linked, you're lying to yourself. A person who is physically healthy but spiritually malnourished will experience unparalleled mental anguish, depression, and hopelessness. Fatigue is one of the most common symptoms of depression. There can also be physical effects (lack of energy), emotional effects (apathy), and cognitive effects (difficulty concentrating).[3]

King Solomon went as far as to say, "All things are wearisome, more than one can say" (Ecclesiastes 1:8 NIV). Tiredness is not a sin. God designed us to get tired, but He also designed us to rest. Tiredness is a symptom, not a disease. When we are physically tired, we must evaluate our lives to locate the cause. Too little sleep? Not eating well? Working too much? Likewise, when we are spiritually tired, we must also take inventory of our actions. Are we resting? Engaging in quiet time? Spending time in His presence? Positioning ourselves to be renewed?

Renewed strength is a promise but not a guarantee. It is conditional and only received in the waiting.

From Waiting to Movement

In *Deutero-Isaiah: A Commentary on Isaiah 40–55*, Klaus Baltzer says this: "As soon as those who 'hope for Yahweh' receive new strength, they begin to move."[4]

It's just like God to leverage waiting into movement. We spend so much time moving in place. We exert a great deal of effort but go nowhere. It's one of the many reasons I hate the treadmill. If I'm going to run that hard for that long, I want to see my surroundings change. God uses waiting as a launching pad. Our movement is no longer reliant on our strength, but His. He becomes the fuel and the fire.

When you feel broken, honor the Sabbath and wait on the Lord. When your thoughts feel fractured, honor the Sabbath and wait on the Lord. When you don't know what to do, honor the Sabbath and wait on the Lord. When you're exhausted, get some sleep, honor the Sabbath, and wait on the Lord. As you do, the miraculous happens. Completeness begins to overflow in your spirit, and you find yourself whole as you (1), God (2), and the Sabbath (3) converge (the impact of biblical numerology is seen once more here). The alignment of the three will never result in stagnation. No, this calibration creates multiplied motivation to move.

During my wife's pregnancy, she would listen to two songs on repeat. One of them was "Take Courage" by Bethel Music.

We waited for Abygail to come, and at the end of the nine months, my wife just wanted the whole ordeal to be over. Every woman who is on that ninth month of pregnancy is shouting, "Amen!" Every night before we fell asleep, we prayed for Abygail. We prayed that the pregnancy would be smooth. We prayed our daughter would be healthy.

If you've read my book *Drift: Finding Your Way Back When Life Throws You Off Course*, you know what happened that fateful delivery day as my wife battled through thirty-six hours of labor. That is a lot of waiting. I believe it was the moments of worship spent in the waiting that gave me the faith to make difficult decisions. I believe it was the waiting that allowed me to worship amid the loss I felt. I believe confidence in His faithfulness was formed in the waiting.

You need to understand, God's promises for your life may be in fetal form right now. They are not yet birth-ready. We cannot speed up God's plan or His process; He disburses exactly what is needed when it's needed. Pursuing a premature promise will lead us to a prison of pain, not a palace of peace. Sometimes all we can do is actively wait.

Despite what some may say, time is not our enemy, and waiting is not a punishment. Time is our opportunity. While Abygail was being formed in my wife's womb, we actively waited. We went to every class we could. (Although there were a couple I truly wish I had skipped. I still have nightmares.)

I learned how to swaddle. I practiced in the waiting and became quite good at it. My wife? Her swaddle skills were suspect. I read books in the waiting, ranging from how to care for my wife in various stages of the pregnancy to principles of raising a kingdom kid. Abygail was not yet born and I prayed for her

Chasing Rabbits

spouse. We played worship music constantly, and I spoke to her nightly. When she was born, she knew Daddy's voice and responded to me when I spoke. I actively waited, and He was in the waiting.

The Sabbath forces us to wait, entrusting the fulfillment of the promise into God's hands and not our own. In fact, God doesn't even need to lift His hands to fulfill His promise. With a spoken word from the Creator, something is formed out of nothing, substance without toil, perfection without pain. He actively creates as we actively wait.

You may insist you're incapable of waiting. You may even tout impatience as a badge of honor and accomplishment; however, if you are aligned with the Spirit of God, patience is the outcome. It's the fruit that comes from intimacy with Him (see Galatians 5:22). This concept is an intense struggle for the Type A personality. Surrendering production to the unseen feels wrong. Since you are God's creation and He is perfect, you cannot claim creative error. We are all created with the capacity to wait, but it is not until we understand the spiritual implications of waiting that we find joy in it.

When you live perpetually impatient, you insist you are on the offensive, conquering foes and taking ground for the kingdom of God. But in His upside-down kingdom, truth is found in the opposite. You will be active but not fruitful. Only in His presence can stillness produce a harvest and patience win wars. It's better to wait on the God of your salvation (see Micah 7:7), because only He can create from nothing. Commerce and consumables carry a net weight of zero in the kingdom of God. All the power you could muster in a hundred years can be undone by

Chasing Rabbits

one word from the Father. Why kick against the goads (see Acts 26:14)?

Forced Waiting

Do you know what's worse than waiting? Forced waiting. It's one thing to volunteer your time. It is vastly different when it's demanded of you. For instance, have you ever had to visit a DMV?

The national average time to receive service at a DMV is forty-four minutes.[5] Forty-four excruciating, mind-numbing minutes. But we wait, and while we may occasionally complain, our dissatisfaction doesn't compel the staff to move any faster. The DMV is not concerned with customer service because they don't have to worry about market share, competitor analysis, or losing a dedicated client. We are required by law to use their services.

Several factors lead to forced waiting. The first is physical exhaustion. The human body can only take so much. It will inevitably demand rest after seasons of prolonged effort. At first, we may reject its demands, but our body will respond with a lower immune system welcoming sickness. According to the Mayo Clinic, "Studies show that people who don't get quality sleep or enough sleep are more likely to get sick after being exposed to a virus, such as a common cold virus. Lack of sleep can also affect how fast you recover if you do get sick."[6] There's nothing like a good virus to force rest.

The second factor is trauma. A failing marriage, troubled children, or the loss of a job can be debilitating and will force us to wait and evaluate. These important areas now demand our attention so forcefully that everything else has to stop if we hope to salvage what's left. Going bowling with friends hardly seems important when our child is battling drug addiction.

The third factor is eternal timing. This factor is laughably beyond our control. God will do what God will do. He cannot be manipulated into movement, but if we want to hear from Him, we'll need to practice waiting. This means forcing ourselves to wait when everything within us screams for activity. This waiting doesn't have to be passive. We can wisely choose active waiting.

Now, how do we actively wait for God? Three Ws: worship, word, and wonder.

Worship while you wait. Worship is a beautiful part of the Sabbath rest. Worship distracts our thoughts from carnal things and places them where they belong. We demote ourselves from being the self-proclaimed center of the universe, and acknowledge the mystery and majesty of Jesus. We exalt who He is above what we want. If you're tired of waiting, worship. Worship until you understand your role in eternity. Worship until He alone becomes the object of you desire.

Then study His *Word*. Actively engage your intellect through hermeneutical practice. Don't just read His Word, study it. Grab a commentary and dig deeper. Learn about historical context, authorship, and geographical influences on Scripture.

Finally, *wonder*. When was the last time you gave your imagination permission to just wonder? When was the last time you allowed yourself to be curious, thinking about things that had no immediate bearing on your present? What if this time of wonder could be divinely guided? Christian mystics have long practiced the soul's union with God and the transformative presence of God.

Chasing Rabbits

Revelation and curiosity are inextricably linked. As we ponder God's grandeur, we can't help but respond with awe. The psalmist declared, "The whole earth is filled with awe at your wonders; where morning dawns, where evening fades, you call forth songs of joy" (Psalm 65:8 NIV).

When you're forcefully waiting, yet expectant for the time when He performs wondrous acts (see Exodus 15:11), it is wise to seek His face, not just His hand. King David exhorts this:

"My heart says of you, 'Seek his face!' Your face, Lord, I will seek" (Psalm 27:8 NIV).

But why forcefully wait at all? Why must we always be backed into a corner, stripped of all other options, before we choose the correct one? What if we chose to wait through patient observance of the Sabbath?

Impatience is a dysfunctional need to control what was never stewarded to us. With forced waiting and active waiting, one chooses us and the other is chosen by us. We desire credit for our activity while God delights in our active waiting. The past version of us who achieved and successfully hunted the rascally rabbit now longs for a resurrection, but we mustn't let the trophies of past hunts adorn our walls without understanding who gave us the strength to pull the trigger.

Chasing Rabbits

MALNOURISHED

CHAPTER SIX

"There is another kind of poverty that only rich men know, a moral malnutrition that starves their very souls."
– Glenn Frey

The desert cottontail is native to the Southwest region of the United States. I feel sorry for these lanky little rabbits, as they are quite pitiful looking. Compared to rabbits in other parts of the world, where the land is lush and there's plenty of vegetation to feed on, the rabbits in the Southwest are all skin and bones, often weighing only one to two pounds.

By contrast, the Flemish Giant rabbit can grow to two and a half feet long and weigh nearly fifteen pounds. This breed originated in Belgium and England but made its way to the United States in the late 1800s. Some people have been known to mistake a Flemish Giant for a small dog. They are prized for their meat and their fur.

If you were to place a malnourished desert cottontail next to a Flemish Giant, there would be no mistaking which had been raised in a more favorable region of the world. There would also be no mistake which one you would take home to make a nice rabbit stew.

Much like a desert rabbit scrounging to find vegetation in a parched land, failure to observe the Sabbath will eventually give way to a malnourished soul, mind, and body. Malnourishment leads to desperation, which is rooted in fear. Fear of poverty can lead someone to work seventy to eighty hours a week and neglect their familial responsibilities. Fear of being alone can lead to relational desperation, taking the form of clinginess, co-dependence, and manipulation. You will always find desperation living next door to its best friend, fear.

The Dangers of Burnout

I tend to be a workaholic, but not because I find my value in work. I simply really enjoy what I do. Yet, in the midst of a particularly busy season, I found myself exhausted. I had worked for about two months without a break. No Sabbath, no vacation, no time off, just work. It was in this season I stumbled upon an article that highlighted ten warning signs pointing to burnout.

I checked off nine out of ten.

In a matter of minutes I felt exhausted, overwhelmed, and apathetic. It wasn't because I read the article; it was because I'd avoided the reality that I could actually burn out. I had always thought burnout was for those who couldn't cut it. It was an excuse to not work hard, not strive, not push forward no matter the cost.

I was so wrong.

After reading the article, I texted my spiritual father, Pastor Rob, and shared how I was feeling. He asked me to come to his house. The lump in my throat grew larger. I began talking to myself. "Why are you feeling this way? GET YOUR ACT TOGETHER!"

As I pulled up to his house, I told myself, "This is good. You're fine. Just stay composed." The pep talk didn't work. I cracked a few jokes as I walked in, still convincing myself this wasn't a big deal. We sat down at his dining room table and he asked, "What's going on, son?"

I broke down, weeping with my head in my hands. I don't know what came over me. It was as if a dam had ruptured in my spirit and every bit of fatigue, frustration, and anxiety I had pushed down for years came flooding out. I felt embarrassed. I felt ashamed. I felt like I had let him down and that I couldn't cut it. Of course, none of those feelings came from the Lord.

After I got it out of my system, Pastor Rob did what any spiritual father would. He affirmed, he comforted, and he put together a plan where I could find some reprieve. This was over a decade ago, and I've had a lot of time to analyze that moment. In hindsight, I had a lot on my plate, but that's not what caused this breakdown. I was malnourished. I was exhausted because in my striving I had relied on carnal fuel to energize me in a spiritual battle. The solution wasn't less work; it was more of God.

Operating in a malnourished state is just as common in Christianity as it is in the secular environment. We try to spiritualize our rebellion under the guise of kingdom promotion, but the Lord sees through it all. It's selfish ambition, and He'll have none of it.

It took a breakdown moment for me to re-evaluate my priorities. I wish I could say everything was perfect from then on out, but to this day I struggle with turning off the phone, closing the laptop, and sitting calmly in His presence during my Sabbath.

I must confess, I should be sleeping right now. It's 12:22 a.m. and I'm plucking away at my computer in an attempt to fulfill a self-imposed deadline to finish this book. But today is not my Sabbath. Sure, you could question my time management, but you won't find me working on my Sabbath.

When people I lead message me on my Sabbath, I still feel guilty for not responding right away. Will they think I'm brushing them off? Will they think I'm a bad leader? Will they lose faith in me? Will they think I'm lazy?

Nonsense.

The right questions are, Will they see health modeled in me? Will they recognize the importance of rest? Will they learn to honor someone's commitment to obey the Lord? Will they feel empowered to rest as well? Will they see the love and grace and compassion of Jesus in the beauty of the Sabbath?

Endless Production

If the Sabbath feels like a burden and you're ready to forgo God's command for the sake of advancement, not only will you end up exhausted and defeated, but you'll also have aligned yourself with the system of this world, the system of the enemy, the system of oppression and slavery.

In his iconic book, *Sabbath as Resistance: Saying No to the Culture of Now*, Walter Brueggemann says,

> Endless production. Into this system of hopeless weariness erupts the God of the burning bush (Exod. 3:1–6). That God heard the despairing fatigue of the slaves (2:23–25), resolved to liberate the slave company of Israel from the exploitative system (3:7–9, and recruited Moses for the human task of emancipation (3:10). The reason Miriam and the other women can sing and dance at the end of the exodus narrative is the emergence of a new social reality in which the life of the Israelite economy is no longer determined and compelled by the insatiable production quotas of Egypt and its gods (15:20–21).[1]

If this was the time of the Exodus, you would have aligned with Pharoah. You would have been the recipient of the plagues. You would have been the taskmaster. Just consider Exodus 5:4: "But the king of Egypt said to them, 'Moses and Aaron, why do you take the people away from their work? Get back to your burdens.'"

There is no rest in the governmental system of this world. Rest is condemned. We even popularize a series of hashtags to show everyone how hard we are working.

#RiseandGrind
#Hustle
#Mindset
#Entrepreneur
#HustleforthatMuscle

We live in a culture where rest is tolerated, not celebrated. We praise the person who sleeps on a futon at work for four hours, neglects their family, and never leaves their office. We put that person on the cover of magazines. We laud them for their inspired technological advancements and business acumen. We celebrate their great buildings, their pyramids, and their monuments.

We extol their imbalance and their dysfunction. We passively ignore their broken homes and their public divorces. We have openly accepted harsh work environments and poor staff culture because we are the beneficiaries of their hard work. This is why the native Egyptians felt no need to start a hashtag movement for the abused Israelites. There were no protests on the royal palace lawn. No statues, shrines, or representations of the over 1,400 gods worshipped in Egypt were torn down for the sake of equality. They benefited from the acts of slavery just as the plantation owners in the Confederate South. Acquire at all costs, even if it requires the abuse of another.

Even if it requires that we abuse ourselves.

Trauma can be cyclical. I don't know that slavery will ever go away. Not as long as profit is to be made from the incessant work of another. Generational abuse victims don't know how to break the cycle.

In his powerful book, *The Body Keeps the Score: Brain, Mind, and Body in the Healing of Trauma*, Bessel A. van der Kolk notes,

> We have learned that trauma is not just an event that took place sometime in the past; it is also the imprint left by that experience on mind, brain, and body. This imprint has ongoing consequences for how the human organism manages to survive in the present. Trauma results in a fundamental reorganization of the way mind and brain manage perceptions. It changes not only how we think and what we think about, but also our very capacity to think.[3]

It takes a renewed mind, and nobody renews the mind like Jesus. The renewed mind protects and defends. The renewed mind is a balanced mind that refuses to serve two masters. The renewed mind does not place mammon over moments. Yet even the renewed mind deteriorates under the weight of exhaustion and spiritual malnourishment. Every concession, no matter how minute, moves us one step closer to the person who would require bricks be made without straw, results without reprieve.

Spiritual Malnourishment

Exhaustion causes us to do very stupid things. In a malnourished state, we will willingly give away our convictions and our inheritance. Pastor and author Carey Nieuwhof says, "Exhaustion is the gateway drug for moral failure."[2]

Exhaustion affects our decision-making. It affects our relationships. It is a breeding ground for bitterness, resentment, and a forfeited future. No Bible story illustrates this better than that of Jacob and Esau.

> Once when Jacob was cooking stew, Esau came in from the field, and he was exhausted. And Esau said to Jacob, "Let me eat some of that red stew, for I am exhausted!" (Therefore his name was called Edom.) Jacob said, "Sell me your birthright now." Esau said, "I am about to die; of what use is a birthright to me?" Jacob said, "Swear to me now." So he swore to him and sold his birthright to Jacob. Then Jacob gave Esau bread and lentil stew, and he ate and drank and rose and went his way. Thus Esau despised his birthright. (Genesis 25:29–34)

Esau planned his schedule poorly. He didn't allow for margin. He took his body to the limits, and in a malnourished state gave away his blessing. His malnourishment led to desperation. Desperation is rooted in fear.

In his article "Overcoming Depression and Desperation in the time of COVID-19," Dr. Gregory Jantz noted, "For many, I would include desperation and a byproduct during the depression phase. We can become desperate when things seem out of our control—our finances, our health, our relationships."[3]

Dr. Jantz describes a chaotic world wherein the things that should be within some realm of control are unpredictable and unstable. It's Egypt. It's toil without end, without advancement, without peace. It's work without hope. It's being financially broke at the end of an eighty-hour work week. It's being relationally bankrupt because work has monopolized our time and robbed those we love from intimacy with us. It's our children knowing of us and loving the idea of us, but at the end of the day they're more familiar with their friends, coworkers, and teachers than they are with us. We sacrifice our health and relationships for a financial blessing that will never satisfy us. It's Egypt on repeat.

Really, if we confess faith in Jesus, shouldn't we put more trust in the all-knowing creator of the universe? Wouldn't we resist submitting ourselves to the emotional, physical, and relational slavery of Egypt? Regarding this, Brueggeman comments,

> At the taproot of this divine commitment to relationship (covenant) rather than commodity (bricks) is the capacity and willingness of this God to rest. The Sabbath rest of God is the acknowledgment that God and God's people in the world are not commodities to be dispatched for endless production and so dispatched, as we used to say, as "hands" in the service of a command economy. Rather they are subjects situated in an economy of neighborliness. All of that is implicit in the reality and exhibit of divine rest.[4]

Capacity. Neighborliness. Covenant. Relationship. Rest. This sounds ... right.

God is not depending on us to maintain His creation with unceasing activity. And even if He was, would we be able to maintain very long in a malnourished state? We'd be desert cottontails in a land of Flemish Giants, always more concerned about surviving than thriving.

Working from the Sabbath

When my wife and I were planning our lives together, she

insisted we take a yearly vacation. "I work for vacation," she would say. For her, the vacation was the prize at the end of the race, but this is not the case with the Sabbath. We do not work *toward* the Sabbath. We work *from* the Sabbath.

If we worked toward the Sabbath, we would be Esau in the biblical narrative. If Esau had been wise, he would've set up camp at a designated location and retreated there often for supplies while he hunted. And if that range wasn't yielding the food he needed, he would've repositioned camp and tried again, never being too far from a place of rest. Instead he overestimated his own capacity and found himself in a place of desperation, willing to give everything that mattered to him to regain his strength.

When we work toward the Sabbath, we allow our work to dictate the occurrence of the Sabbath, and if the work is not completed, we continue to shift the Sabbath forward until the work is done. But the work is never done, so the Sabbath becomes a mechanical lure on a dog track that we can never catch. It keeps moving and we keep chasing, but we never find satisfaction; we never feast on the catch. And if by chance the moment comes when we do catch what we're chasing, because we're working toward rest and not from rest, it will never satisfy. Our dysfunction will be rewarded and lead to more dysfunction. Our win will positively reinforce bad behavior.

Alice Boyes of the *Harvard Business Review* published an article online called "Resisting the Pressure to Overwork." Regarding learned work behavior she comments,

> Here's a very basic law of psychology: When behaviors are reinforced, they increase. When you ignore them, you might see an "extinction burst"—a short-term rise in the problematic

behaviors—but then they will stop. For example, if a colleague emails you after-hours and you reply, you're encouraging more work at night. The sender will ask for more—from you and everyone else. If you instead ignore inappropriate attempts to push you to overwork, the person may for a short period of time try frenetically and in more manipulative ways to get you to comply—the extinction burst—but then they'll adapt. People are wired to learn.[5]

When we work from the Sabbath, we're moving from a place of completion. It's not a completion of work; it's a completion found in the unity with God we experience in the place of rest. It's the moment when every incomplete, malnourished thought and emotion is filtered through perfect love and grace from a perfect Father who knows exactly what we need. In this metaphysical moment, we transcend what the world celebrates. The grind. The hustle. The comparison. None of it matters in His presence because we are fully accepted just as we are in that moment. His love rains down in torrents, and the spiritual nourishment we receive allows us to work six days from a place of spiritual conclusion.

As we work from the Sabbath, we near the end of the week with joy and expectation, not loathing, as we think of our long list of unchecked boxes. We end our six days of effort with anticipation because we know we will soon feast on the spiritual, emotional, relational, and psychological buffet of the Sabbath.

Esau was a skilled hunter, and he lived with the same motto as those who work in sales: You eat what you kill. He didn't kill, so he had nothing to eat, and because he was not successful, he became willing to sacrifice his future for food. Today, we operate

Chasing Rabbits

with the same sense of urgency. We work to kill, and when we don't kill, we fear we won't eat. We don't want to be Esau. We don't want to be the man who was not concerned with his future, only the present.

Look what happened to Esau next: "And Esau said to Jacob, 'Let me eat some of the red stew, for I am exhausted!' Jacob said, 'Sell me your birthright now.' Esau said, 'I am about to die, of what use is a birthright to me?'" (Genesis 25:31–32)

Jacob, the deceiver, seemingly represents the demand of this world. "Give me everything that's valuable to you," it screams, "and I will nourish you." As we discover in the story of Jacob and Esau, there's always a reckoning. There's always a moment when we realize the decisions we made in the past have caused pain in the present.

When we neglect the Sabbath, we neglect ourselves, our families, our friends, and our relationship with God. Things may go well for a season, but when pressured, the emaciated soul will always give what it holds most valuable to stay alive for one more day. It will give away a marriage, children, morality, or principles under the guise of provision.

Yet, if we haven't eaten, what strength do we have to give? Jesus proclaimed, "I am the bread of life. Whoever comes to me will never go hungry, and whoever believes in me will never be thirsty. But as I told you, you have seen me and still you do not believe" (John 6:35–36 NIV).

Is this promise not enough? Is a satisfied life not attractive? Is fulfillment so repulsive that it must come secondary to momentary happiness? Accepting Jesus's invitation brings us into an intimate, enveloping presence where all our ambition for accumulation slips away and we find ourselves eating of bread we

Chasing Rabbits

didn't make and drinking water we didn't pour, and here lies one of the eternal mysteries of the Sabbath: If we slow down enough to meet with Him, we'll find He has already prepared the table.

His supply is limitless, and non-discriminatory. *Whoever comes.* Whoever comes will not be turned away. Whoever comes has a chance to encounter the risen Savior. Whoever comes has the opportunity to be refreshed by living water and comforted by the peacemaker. "The Sabbath was made for man, not man for the Sabbath," Jesus declared (Mark 2:27 NIV).

He created the stoppage of industry for the sweetness of intimacy around a table of divine conversation.

Perhaps, at this table, there would also be rabbit stew.

Chasing Rabbits

SHABBAT SHALOM

CHAPTER SEVEN

"God cannot give us a happiness and peace apart from Himself, because it is not there."
– C. S. Lewis

Rabbits are easily scared. Rapid movements, escalated voices, and loud noises can signal danger to the rabbit. They act as if a predator is near. They are skittish and afraid.

Sometimes humans act like rabbits. Any slight deviation from our desired routine, schedule, or outcome throws us into turmoil. As much as we'd like to label this a Gen-Z trait, humanity has been averse to uncertainty since the garden. Knowing what is to come brings peace and comfort like a heavy blanket on a wintry night. Uncertainty makes us jumpy like a victim in a horror movie—prone to run upstairs, trip, fall, and still end up face-to-face with the boogeyman.

Our level of spiritual engagement directly affects how we accept negative circumstances. In a study titled "Peace, Equanimity, and Acceptance in the Cancer Experience: Validation of a scale to assess acceptance and struggle with terminal illness," researchers found there's a notable increase in end-of-life acceptance scores based on spiritual engagement. In other words, the more spiritual the person, the greater the peace when receiving a terminal diagnosis.[1]

It shouldn't come as a surprise to the followers of Jesus that spiritual engagement brings peace during troubled times. What should come as a surprise is how seldom we lean into this peace. Our complaints carry the sound of a skipping record. It's annoying, yes, but until we choose to life the needle the irritating sound of our complaining voices will resume.

Why does spirituality matter? If you haven't lived your life as if God existed prior to turmoil, how could you miraculously find tranquility in His presence now? This serenity has less to do with us and more to do with His eternal kindness. Even if rejected for a lifetime, God holds fast to His promise to never leave and forsake us. He fulfills His word to give transcendent peace to those who make their requests to Him.

The greater question is, why wait? Why does it take tragedy for us to receive peace? Ralph Waldo Emerson once said, "Nobody can bring you peace but yourself."[2] Emerson may have been a revolutionary poet, but he couldn't have been more wrong about this. There is a constant war between our soul and spirit. The only way to escape that fight is death, unless someone who stands outside our inner turmoil is able to impart something supernatural into the equation that's strong enough to quell dissension. Emerson did get it right, however, when he said, "For everything you gain, you lose something."[3] If we want to gain peace, we need to loosen our grip on what's known. Peace requires a substantial amount of faith in the unseen. Hebrews 11:1 says, "Faith is confidence in what we hope for and assurance about what we do not see" (NIV).

If you want peace, it may be best to close your eyes to everything around you, including your convoluted solutions. Enter your Sabbath rest with curiosity, not entitlement. You'll find yourself oddly surprised, excited, and rejuvenated. The unknown will now be the beginning of your next great adventure with Jesus.

Two Types of Peace

Jesus delivered uncanny clarity in John 14:27: "I am leaving you with a gift—peace of mind and heart. And the peace I give is a gift the world cannot give. So don't be troubled or afraid" (NLT).

According to Jamieson, Faust, and Brown,

Chasing Rabbits

It is a parting word, but of richest import, the customary "peace" of a parting friend sublimed and transfigured. As "the Prince of Peace" (Is 9:6) He brought it into flesh, carried it about in His Own Person ("My peace") died to make it ours, left it as the heritage of His disciples upon earth, implants and maintains it by His Spirit in their hearts. Many a legacy is "left" that is never "given" to the legatee, many a gift destined that never reaches its proper object. But Christ is the Executor of His own Testament; the peace He "leaves" He "gives."[4]

We can infer that there are two types of peace. The peace the world gives is partial and unfulfilling; it is temporal and limited. This type of "peace" will change like the seasons. What once brought peace may now bring turmoil. This is the peace the world gives. It comes when there is no more war to be had, but it only exists as a placeholder for the next turmoil. The world's peace comes through violence and manipulation. When the world gives peace, there is always a catch, always a hidden agenda, always an ulterior motive.

Then there is the peace Jesus gives. A perfect peace available to all, it is consistent, abundant, and free. It is the peace of the Sabbath. It doesn't exist after the turbulence. It exists *within* the turbulence. The world can give war or peace, but not both at the same time.

Bible scholar D. A. Carson notes,

> At the individual level, this peace secures composure in the midst of trouble, and dissolves fear, as the final injunction of this verse demonstrates. This is the peace which garrisons our hearts and minds against the invasion of anxiety (Phil. 4:7), and rules or arbitrates in the hearts of God's people to main-

tain harmony amongst them (Col. 3:15). When we choose a Sabbath rest we answer God's as He beckons us to receive peace. Hebrews 4:9–10 encourages, "There remains, then, a Sabbath-rest for the people of God; for anyone who enters God's rest also rests from their works, just as God did from his."[5]

Daily Intimacy with God

Introductions can be awkward. Few would associate the interaction with someone new as peaceful. Most of us just want to get out of the conversation as quickly as possible before it gets weird. Believe it or not, researchers have studied this interaction and coined it *uncertainty reduction theory* (URT).

URT was originally created to explain the communication process that occurs when two strangers interact. In 1975, Charles Berger and Richard Calabrese observed that when we interact with strangers, we experience uncertainty because we don't really know what to expect. Berger and Calabrese claim that as the interaction proceeds, we gain information that quickly reduces our uncertainties.[6]

However, there have probably been times when you didn't really worry about finding out anything about the stranger because you never expected to see the person again or it wasn't someone with whom you wanted to pursue a relationship. URT provides explanations for these and other behaviors when people interact with someone new.

With this in mind, could this negative feeling be a reason why someone avoids the Sabbath? Is it awkward to talk to God because we don't have a personal relationship with Him? Are we uncertain of who He is, and that uncertainty repels us from the Sabbath?

Author Mark Buchanan says, "Too much work, the British used to say, makes Jack a dull boy. But it's worse than that. It numbs Jack, parches Jack, hardens Jack. It kills his heart. When we get too busy, everything becomes either a trudge or a scramble, the doldrums or sheer mayhem. We get bored with the familiar, threatened by the unfamiliar. We just want to be left alone. Busyness kills the heart."7

God is the God of the Sabbath, but He is also God during the other six days. He set aside the Sabbath for our fragile frames, but He desires a daily relationship.

If we've ignored daily intimacy, then we won't give the Sabbath a second thought. But if we speak with Him daily in the middle of working, creating, and forming the world around us, an entire day with Him would feel like a dream come true.

So if our faithful steps and intimate pursuits lead us to the place where He is with us (see Isaiah 41:10; Joshua 1:9; Zephaniah 3:17; Matthew 28:20; Hebrews 13:5; Psalm 23:4; James 4:8), we will find peace. Jesus's very name signifies His desire: "'Behold, a virgin shall conceive and bear a son, and they shall call his name Immanuel' (which means, God with us)" (Matthew 1:23).

He will be with us. He promised. Getting what we want is not an indicator of His presence or faithfulness. Bad times are not proof of His absence, and great times are not proof of His nearness. He is near, always. And when He is near, we have the beautiful opportunity to envelop our worries with peace that transcends understanding.

Pursuing True Peace

In Isaiah 26:12, the prophet proclaims, "Lord, you establish peace for us; all that we have accomplished, you have done for us" (NIV). We work so hard to be "at peace," when as believers we should live "within peace."

Peace is one of the desired benefits to incessant work. We so desire the absence of strife and complications that we'll complicate our lives and stir up strife to get there. Long hours at work produce endless tension at home. Arguments ensue as we miss school plays, games, anniversaries, dinners, and a litany of other memorable moments all in the name of providing for those moments.

Peace feels like chasing a mechanical rabbit around the track. We feel like we can see it, sometimes almost touch it, but we never catch it, at least not for any significant amount of time. We never truly feel at peace. There is always something waiting to fill the white space on our calendars, but those lingering commitments are never the valuable ones.

Ask yourself this: When was the last time I scheduled an entire day on my calendar for intimacy with God? When was the last time He took precedence over a bigger paycheck or temporal accomplishment?

We feel like we must fight to gain peace. I disagree. Internal peace isn't ours to earn; it's ours to receive. Instead, we must fight to find the appropriate position to receive peace. If peace was something we could earn with our own strength, then it would suddenly take the shape of the mechanical lure on a dog track. It would be just another to-do on our list instead of something to experience in His presence.

Isaiah 26:3 informs us of the conditions wherein God distributes peace: "You will keep in perfect peace those whose minds are steadfast, because they trust in you" (NIV). He establishes perfect peace by His hands and provides it as some sort of spiritual bubble for those whose attention, thoughts, and passions are consistently focused on Him. What a marvelous gift!

We must not corner our thinking into defining peace according to our own standards. Peace is not the absence of hostility. The nature of peace with God is evidently glorious and much more than the absence of hostility—for peace is parallel with good things (see Deuteronomy 23:6; Ezra 9:12), such as:

- Inheriting the land (Psalm 37:11)
- Long life (Proverbs 3:2)
- Quietness and trust (Isaiah 32:17–18)
- Righteousness (Psalms 35:27; 37:37; 72:3; 85:10; Isaiah 48:18; 60:17)
- Strength (Psalm 29:11)
- Tranquility (Genesis 15:15; Exodus 18:23; 2 Kings 2:6; Psalm 4:8; Isaiah 32:17)
- Divine steadfast love (Jeremiah 16:5)

Peace is not achieved through financial prosperity. The Bible is clear there is a time for peace, as there is a time for war. It cannot be manipulated or independently manifested. Peace is a break in the cycle of war and aggression.

Yet, we are confused. We desire peace but we reject the Sabbath, the one day God gave us to love our neighbor, remove ourselves from the hamster wheel, and focus on Him. The Sabbath brings the perfect future into the imperfect present.

Chasing Rabbits

One of the most alluring elements of heaven is not the gold streets or pearly gates. No, one of the most desired outcomes is peace. No more tears, no more pain, no more suffering, no hurting back or trick knees. No family fights, work tension, or financial stress. It's all gone when we get to heaven. We'll have . . . peace.

"Shabbat Shalom" is a common greeting on the Sabbath. It translates to "peaceful Sabbath," or a "peace-filled day of rest."

That sounds pretty amazing.

External and Internal Tyrannies

Two forms of tyranny are associated with the Exodus and the subsequent commands given to God's people. The first is external (Pharaoh), and the second is internal (self). While the Israelites lived in Egypt, Pharaoh enforced an external tyranny. He did everything he could to impose his rule on the people, even if it meant murdering children. Even if it meant ordering other people to murder children. How heinous was this Pharaoh who was so insistent on maintaining his rule that even the innocent were intentionally targeted. There were no protests or social media justice warriors to question his rule. The people knew better. Their punishment would not be something as passive-aggressive as being banned from the internet. No, their punishment would be immediate death.

This was the arena from which God pulled His people. It was a place of constant oppression, exhaustion, and fear. And it was considered normal. In fact, it was preferred over bearing the responsibility of freedom. Even when Moses came, their response was laughably dysfunctional.

Chasing Rabbits

Internal tyranny is arguably much harder to overcome. When Pharaoh commanded the Israelites to make brick without straw, they responded, "Then the Israelite overseers went and appealed to Pharaoh: 'Why have you treated your servants this way?'" (Exodus 5:15 NIV).

Your servants. Not *God's servants* or *Pharaoh's servants.* After hundreds of years of cruelty, they associated more closely with Pharaoh than with Yahweh, and this association was harder to break than they expected. There is no doubt they hated Pharaoh and the fact that they had to withstand his dictatorship to survive, but it seems they equally hated their new liberator. No, not Moses, but God. It seemed inconceivable that He would care for them, love them, and lead them with no ulterior motive. Perhaps they believed they simply moved from one dictator to another, and it was only a matter of time before He let them down.

Then God cracked His metaphorical knuckles and parted a sea. He provided a supernatural GPS system in the form of a cloud by day and a fire by night. He made an incredibly merciful gesture to prove that He was not the same as Pharaoh: "Take the day off. That's right. Not one day a month, no. Take one day off every single week forever. And better yet, by taking this one day off, you'll be more blessed than if you had worked." One might think this would cement the relational deal, but it didn't.

I'd love to say we learned our lesson over thousands of years and that the careful observance of the Sabbath has been emphatically proven, but we're just as hesitant with God's benevolence now as we've ever been. The peace should have been settled when the tyrannical ruler had been neutralized.

It turns out that was the easy part. The tyranny of self lives on.

Chasing Rabbits

IT'S ABOUT TIME

CHAPTER EIGHT

*"Time stays long enough for anyone who will use it.
– Leonardo Da Vinci*

It's about time is a double entendre. Yes, it's about time <u>we</u> observed the Sabbath, and observing the Sabbath is about time.

When I was in my late twenties, I took a course called Life Management Study (LMS). It was the most impactful course I'd ever taken, based on the book, *It's About Time* by Ken Smith. The thirteen-week course was created to help realign people to God's priorities.

As a pastor, I can say that most of my spiritual counseling sessions begin with questions about priorities. Nearly every conflict is marred by people who have lost sight of what matters—by people who have been chasing rabbits.

In his book *Take the Day Off*, Robert Morris notes, "Once you begin the process of transferring your priorities, values, and goals from your heart to your calendar, you're going to be presented with a set of difficult choices. . . . In other words, saying yes to the things that are most important will almost certainly require saying no to several, perhaps many, worthwhile things. This is a potentially painful but very healthy, vitally important process."[1]

The Sabbath doesn't occur by accident and neither do healthy priorities. We may feel it's unfair to have to restrain ourselves to someone else's opinion of how to spend our time. But it's not our time. The prophet Jeremiah declared, "I know, Lord, that our lives are not our own. We are not able to plan our own course" (Jer. 10:23 NLT). And the apostle Paul affirmed, "You are not your own, you were bought with a price. Therefore honor God with your bodies" (1 Corinthians 6:19–20 NIV).

When we give God one day of the week by refraining from work and entering into His rest, we are not giving Him something that is ours. Much like the tithe, we are returning to Him

Chasing Rabbits

what is already His. It is holy. It is *His* day. We should no more rob Him of His day than we should rob Him of His tithe.

"But what about Jesus?" some people say. "Isn't Jesus the fulfillment of the Sabbath?" When we enter into the Sabbath rest, we enter into the rest of Jesus. Hebrews 4:3 indicates that those who have believed enter that rest. What did they believe in? Jesus. Jesus's words in Matthew 11:29–30 prophetically speak of what was and what would be: "Take my yoke upon you, and learn from me, for I am gentle and lowly in heart, and you will find rest for your souls. For my yoke is easy, and my burden is light."

When we find Jesus, we find rest, yet too many believers refuse the rest Jesus offers. It's not that we don't look for this rest; it's just that we look in the wrong places. If we truly believe our rest is found in Him, then it's about time we apply action to our belief. How do we apply action to our belief? Let's look at some ways.

Anticipate the Sabbath

I remember as a child being excited for Christmas morning. Perhaps you shared this feeling. I couldn't sleep as I envisioned tearing through the packages and playing with shiny new toys. I just knew my life would be better the moment Christmas morning arrived.

One could argue that every day is a gift. I agree. But I don't receive gifts every day. Christmas just felt special, and it still does. I now view the Sabbath the same way. Six days of my week are a gift, and I try to make each day count, but man do I look forward to my Sabbath. I practice my Sabbath on Fridays, and on Thursday night I get a little giddy. I start to think about my Sabbath rest, about listening to my Father's voice, being refreshed by the Holy Spirit. I look forward to moments of solitude, of reading a book, of going to lunch with my wife. It's a day when I. Don't. Work. To work may be obedient to my employer, but it would be disobedient to God. I'll err on the side of pleasing God, thank you.

When you anticipate the Sabbath, you plan for the Sabbath. Much like the kid who thinks about all the things they'll do with their new toys on Christmas morning, so you'll begin to think up ways to delight in His presence.

Create a "So That" List

There was a time I struggled with writing books and creating content. I prefer being behind the scenes, and developing social media posts and videos feels exhausting. I don't enjoy it. I had the wrong perspective, and I lost sight of why I obey Him in the first place. It's "so that"...

- Others can be encouraged in the Lord
- I can help people grow spiritually
- I can empower people to achieve their God-given purpose
- I can better provide for my family and leave an inheritance for my children's children (see Proverbs 13:22)

When it came to the Sabbath, I had to take the same approach. Why Sabbath? "So that"...

- I can have energy to play with my daughter
- I have something to look forward to weekly
- I can grow myself
- I can hear His voice
- I can build intimacy with the one who loves me most
- I can have fun with my family
- I can rest my body and mind
- I can have a hobby
- I can break free from carnal desires
- I can de-emphasize materialism in my life
- I can develop trust in the Lord

Creating a "so that" list will help you stay focused on why you're doing what you're doing in the first place. It will keep your motives clear and your conscience set on Him and the benefits. You'll realize you gain far more than you lose by observing the Sabbath. In time, you'll wonder what you ever did without it.

Sleep

Some people live for sleep. I live for work and productivity. I hate sleeping, and until recently I never took naps (except on Sundays after church, of course). Sleep feels like such an interruption to everything good.

My wife, on the other hand, doesn't share my torturous abhorrence of the time sucker called sleep. She loves sleep. I've never known her to *not* take a nap. She can sleep anytime, anywhere. I'm convinced she could sleep on a bed of thumbtacks in broad daylight at a rock concert.

If you love sleep, the Sabbath is for you. I encourage you to sleep, whether it's for thirty minutes or two hours. Give your body a chance to tell you what it needs. If you hate sleep, the Sabbath is for you. You need to give yourself permission to close your eyes and do nothing. Sleep is not a sin. It's mandatory for us to function at a high level. Maybe you should make it one of your "so that'" statements. You sleep on the Sabbath so that your body and mind are ready for high productivity the next six days. Try it out. What's the worst that could happen? You're not missing out on anything, because the Sabbath is not controlled by external influences. It's for you. So stop, sleep, and don't apologize for doing so.

Create

I recall my father building things out of wood on his day off. He might work on the basement, craft a workbench for the garage, or frame a bookcase for his office. Mom used to gripe, "Honey, you need to rest." She didn't realize he was resting. It was life-giving for him, and it was something he didn't have time for the other six days of the week.

It didn't make sense when I was a child, but then I discovered the joys of working on my car. I love getting greasy and dirty and working on my engine. My mind gets lost in the process, and I could stay in my garage for hours tinkering away.

I'm convinced that observing the Sabbath doesn't mean staring at a wall for eighteen hours. It means doing things that restore your soul. Yes, that starts with intentional time in God's presence, but if I'm honest, I also hear Him pretty loudly as I work on my car. I'm still intentionally listening for Him as I change out my spark plugs.

You may like to draw, paint, or build birdhouses. You may enjoy writing or mowing your grass or planting flowers. Don't do these things because you're obligated to. This isn't the time to cross things off your honey-do list. No, these should be things you want to do and enjoy doing. Create something with your mind and allow your hands to follow suit. It may be creating a cleaner engine or a new oil painting. God won't be offended.

Share with Others

In the Old Testament, the Sabbath was communal and personal. When I began consistently observing the Sabbath, I was selfish. I believed it was all about me and everyone should leave me alone to do what I wanted. For most, this is unrealistic. The Sabbath is about communing with God and communing with others who are of the same heart and mind. Be with those people you enjoy, the people who give you life and make you better. It's okay to protect your time with both.

One area we've attempted is sharing a meal with a family we love being around. It hasn't always worked out and we haven't been consistent in doing so, but there is something special about breaking bread with friends and family.

Fresh Air

If possible, get some fresh air! Go outside and enjoy God's creation. It's an overused cliché, but truly take time to smell the roses. Observe the animals God cares so much about, and remember that He cares even more about you. Enjoy the breeze, the sun, the rain—enjoy it all. There's so much beauty around, but when we're chasing rabbits, we seldom see His splendor. God created our bodies to benefit from being outside. Observing the Sabbath doesn't have to be boring.

Go for a walk in the local park, grab a kayak and paddle around on the river or a lake, head to the beach, or simply sit on your patio. It doesn't cost a dime to walk outside, but it has great benefits. For example, the sun:

- Enhances your mood
- Relieves stress
- Improves sleep
- Boosts vitamin D, which affects bone strength

Reduce Screen Time

This suggestion alone is enough to make some readers grab their torch and pitchfork. Yet, according to the University of Pittsburgh Medical Center, too much screen time affects adults and children alike. It can attribute to:

- Problems sleeping
- Eye strain
- Wrist pain
- Depression
- Weight gain
- Altered brain functioning
- Increased blood pressure
- Poor self-image and body image

Whether you want to hear it or not, your device will not give you peace as you observe the Sabbath. Figure out a family plan. I don't suggest going cold turkey. Start by leaving it in your bedroom for a few hours as you spend the morning with Holy Spirit. Maybe your entire family can put their devices in a basket and turn off the television and learn to enjoy each other again. Will it be hard? Yes. Will you see a difference in your family unity, peace of mind, and mood? Absolutely.

Be Consistent

Observing the Sabbath is a spiritual act, so you can expect your flesh, and the flesh of your family and friends, to convince you to abandon the principle before you even get started. Stay consistent. Have hard conversations. Make a plan. In time, this will be your favorite part of the week.

I suggest creating a routine, a weekly ritual, that you look forward to. If you're married, collaborate with your spouse on what you can do together. Maybe it's a consistent prayer or a location you like to visit. Maybe you eat out on your Sabbath. Whatever it is, be consistent and you'll find yourself not even thinking about what rabbits need to be chased.

SHEPPARTON REVISITED

THE CONCLUSION

There's a part of Ginny Lou the greyhound's story I didn't tell you. Ginny Lou acted instinctively and chased after the real rabbit; however, she eventually ran back onto the track to finish the race with the other dogs, once again chasing the mechanical hare.

The Sabbath is not a one-time thing. While you may be blessed to do it once, if you return to the race, that moment will be a vapor. It will be a fond recollection of that one time you slowed down enough to experience the presence of God and the promise of rest. This isn't God's best for you.

Scott Stefanos, Ginny Lou's trainer, applauded her actions, saying, "To her credit she thought she was doing the right thing, then had the nous to carry on and join the rest of the field."[1]

An abundance of voices will flood your life when you decide to walk in the ways God has commanded. You may be confused as to why so many people hate the fact that you have committed time to God, your friends, and your family one day a week. They may even be offended and threaten to end the friendship.

God loves all His children, but His anointing is not equitable and He is not required to disperse favor to anyone. He does so because He loves us so much. He will draw near to those who draw near to Him, and just as Joseph donned a coat of many colors and was hated by his brothers, so many will be annoyed by you. Observing the Sabbath will unsettle the religious spirit and bring unhealthy critical comments.

Do. It. Anyway. Don't return to the track. Don't start chasing the thing you've tried so hard to leave. Chase the real thing and you'll find yourself declaring to all who will listen, "You make known to me the path of life; you will fill me with joy in

Chasing Rabbits

your presence, with eternal pleasures at your right hand" (Psalm 16:11 NIV). What could be better than that?

Chasing Rabbits

ENDNOTES

CHAPTER 1:
1. Abraham Heschel, *The Sabbath* (New York: Farrar, Straus, and Giroux, 1951), 13.

CHAPTER 2:
1. Ashli Akins, The Creativity of Chaos, https://youtu.be/a3RJ0Yx-RCSg.
2. Jordan Peterson, *12 Rules for Life: An Antidote for Chaos* (Canada: Random House, 2018), 158.
3. https://www.christianitytoday.com/pastors/1981/ summer/eugene-peterson-unbusy-pastor.html.

CHAPTER 3:
1. https://www.barna.com/research/sotb-2021/.
2. Brennan Manning, *The Signature of Jesus* (Colorado Springs: Multnomah Publishing House, 1996).
3. Mother Teresa, *In the Heart of the World: Thoughts, Stories and Prayers* (San Francisco: New World Library, 2010).
4. Ralph Enlow, *"Awe, Awesome,"* in *Evangelical Dictionary of Biblical Theology*, electronic ed., Baker Reference Library (Grand Rapids: Baker Book House, 1996), 46.

CHAPTER 4:
1. Stevens, Janet, and Aesop. *The Tortoise and the Hare: An Aesop Fable.* 1984.
2. Martin J. Selman, *2 Chronicles: An Introduction and Commentary*, vol. 11, Tyndale Old Testament Commentaries (Downers Grove, IL: InterVarsity Press, 1994), 415.
3. Ibid., 416.

CHAPTER 5:
1. https://www.cdc.gov/sleep/data_statistics.html.
2. John Nolland, *The Gospel of Matthew: A Commentary on the Greek Text, New International Greek Testament Commentary* (Grand Rapids, MI; Carlisle: W.B. Eerdmans; Paternoster Press, 2005), 1101.
3. https://share.upmc.com/2020/10/fatigue-and-depression/.
4. Klaus Baltzer, *Deutero-Isaiah: A Commentary on Isaiah 40–55*, ed. Peter Machinist, *Hermeneia—a Critical and Historical Commentary on the Bible* (Minneapolis, MN: Fortress Press, 2001), 84.
5. https://www.mayoclinic.org/diseases-conditions/insomnia/expert-answers/lack-of-sleep/faq-20057757.

CHAPTER 6:
1. https://www.marylandzoo.org/animal/flemish-giant-rabbit/.
2. Walter Brueggemann, *Sabbath As Resistance: Saying No to the Culture of Now* (Louisville: Westminster John Knox Press, 2014), 5.
3. Bessel A. Van der Kolk, *The Body Keeps the Score: Brain, Mind, and Body in the Healing of Trauma* (New York: Viking, 2014).
4. https://careynieuwhof.com/exhaustion-gateway-drug-to-moral-falure/.
5. https://www.psychologytoday.com/us/blog/hope-relationships/202004/overcoming-depression-and-desperation-in-the-time-covid-19.
6. Brueggemann, 6.
7. https://hbr.org/2022/05/resisting-the-pressure-to-overwork?position=9.

CHAPTER 7:
1. https://www.ncbi.nlm.nih.gov/pmc/articles/PMC3809101/.
2. Robert Jamieson, A. R. Fausset, and David Brown, *Commentary Critical and Explanatory on the Whole Bible, vol. 2* (Oak Harbor, WA: Logos Research Systems, Inc., 1997), 156.

3. D. A. Carson, *The Gospel according to John, The Pillar New Testament Commentary* (Leicester, England; Grand Rapids, MI: Inter-Varsity Press; W.B. Eerdmans, 1991), 506.
4. https://dr.lib.iastate.edu/entities/publication/8f725318-911e-41ab-8f3f-a095c24b1ba7.
5. Mark Buchanan, *The Rest of God: Restoring Your Soul by Restoring Sabbath* (Nashville: Thomas Nelson, 2007).
6. Joshua M. Greever, *"Peace,"* ed. John D. Barry et al., The Lexham Bible Dictionary (Bellingham, WA: Lexham Press, 2016).

CHAPTER 8:
1. Robert Morris, Take the Day Off: Receiving God's Gift of Rest (Nashville: FaithWords, 2019), Kindle Edition 137.
2. https://www.webmd.com/a-to-z-guides/ss/slideshow-sunlight-health-effects.

CONCLUSION:
1. https://metro.co.uk/2010/07/21/clever-greyhound-ginny-lou-chases-real-hare-off-track-during-race-at-shepparton-track-455024/.

Chasing Rabbits

Are you resting yet?

MORE FROM TIM TWIGG

Drift: Finding Your Way Back When Life Throws You Off Course

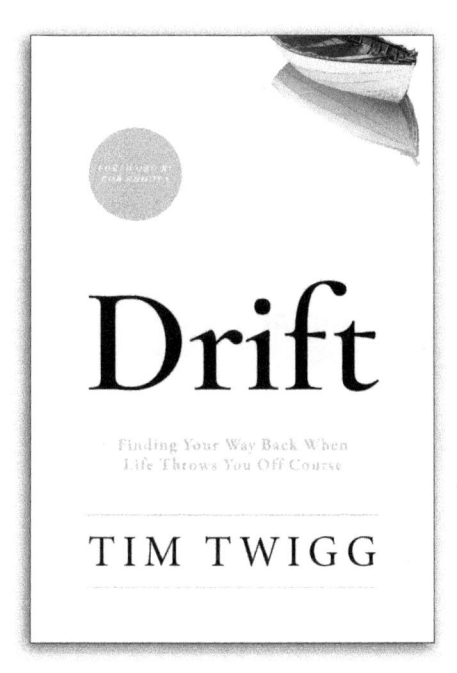

> Many of us are like driftwood, dead but still moving. If you've found yourself in a place you never thought you'd be, this book is for you.

AVAILABLE FOR PURCHASE

BARNES & NOBLE   amazon

www.twtwigg.com

PUBLISH. YOUR. PASSION.

You don't have to be **famous** to be:

PROFOUND
CREATIVE
IMAGINATIVE
INSPIRED

We help authors experience their dream manifested for the world to discover.

www.arrowpresspublishing.com